Are they rich because they're smart?

ALSO BY JACK BARNES

BOOKS & PAMPHLETS
Malcolm X, Black Liberation, and the Road
  to Workers Power (2009)
Cuba and the Coming American Revolution (2007)
The Changing Face of US Politics (2002)
Their Trotsky and Ours (2002)
The Working Class and the Transformation of Learning (2000)
Capitalism's World Disorder (1999)
Malcolm X Talks to Young People (1965)

FROM THE PAGES OF 'NEW INTERNATIONAL'
The Clintons' Antilabor Legacy:
  Roots of the 2008 World Financial Crisis (2008)
Capitalism's Long Hot Winter Has Begun (2005)
Our Politics Start with the World (2005)
US Imperialism Has Lost the Cold War (1998)
The Opening Guns of World War III (1991)
Politics of Economics: Che Guevara and Marxist Continuity (1991)
The Fight for a Workers and Farmers Government in the US (1985)

COLLECTIONS AND INTRODUCTIONS
Teamster Rebellion/Dobbs (2004)
The History of American Trotskyism/Cannon (2002)
The Eastern Airlines Strike/E. Mailhot (1991)
FBI on Trial (1988)

Are they rich because they're smart?

CLASS, PRIVILEGE AND LEARNING UNDER CAPITALISM

JACK BARNES

PATHFINDER
NEW YORK   LONDON   MONTREAL   SYDNEY

EDITED BY: Steve Clark

ISBN 978-1-60488-087-8
Library of Congress Control Number 2016941105

Manufactured in the United States of America

COVER DESIGN: Toni Gorton

COVER PAINTING: *The Crowd*/Crazy Fish Artworks

PATHFINDER
www.pathfinderpress.com
E-mail: pathfinder@pathfinderpress.com

TABLE OF CONTENTS

ABOUT THE AUTHOR

JACK BARNES is national secretary of the Socialist Workers Party. He has been a member of the party's National Committee since 1963 and a national officer since 1969. He is a contributing editor of *New International* magazine.

Barnes joined the Young Socialist Alliance in December 1960, a few months after a trip to Cuba in July and August of that year. Following his return, he helped organize at Carleton College in Minnesota one of the largest and most active campus chapters of the Fair Play for Cuba Committee. In May 1961 he joined the Socialist Workers Party.

Barnes was a central leader of the successful four-year campaign to defend three members of the Young Socialist Alliance in Bloomington, Indiana, indicted in May 1963 for "assembling" to advocate the overthrow of the State of Indiana by force and violence. During this time he was organizer of the Chicago branch of the SWP and the YSA Midwest organizer. In 1965 Barnes was elected YSA national chairman and became director of the SWP and YSA's work to advance the growing movement against the Vietnam War. In January of that year he met twice with Malcolm X for an interview that was published in the *Young Socialist* magazine.

Since the mid-1970s Jack Barnes has led the effort in the Socialist Workers Party, and worked with others worldwide, to build communist parties the large majority of whose members and leaders are industrial workers and trade unionists actively engaged in broad political work that advances along the road to workers power, thus putting an end to the dictatorship of capital.

This political course toward forging parties proletarian both in program and composition is recorded in numerous articles and collections of Barnes's speeches and writings, some of which are listed at the front of the book.

Introduction

> "The struggle for workers power, and the transformation of property relations necessary to open the transition to socialism, are possible only as working people begin transforming ourselves and our attitudes toward life, work, and each other. Only then will we learn what we're capable of becoming."
>
> JACK BARNES

QUESTIONED DURING a December 2015 radio interview about the tens of thousands of workers turning out at rallies for presidential contender Donald Trump, President Barack Obama chalked this up to the fact that "blue-collar men have had a lot of trouble in this new economy, where they are no longer getting the same bargain they got when they were going to a factory and able to support their families on a single paycheck.

"You combine those things," Obama added, "and it means there is going to be potential anger, frustration, fear—some of it justified but just misdirected."

Only in some make-believe past did factory workers in the United States ever receive a "bargain." Workers resisted—and will never stop resisting—abusive treatment on the job. They joined together ever more broadly to organize unions, waged strikes against the employers and the government, and won what they were strong enough to take without organizing on the political level independently from the bosses' parties.

What's most remarkable about Obama's language, however, is not its patronizing tone toward "blue collar men." It's the *fear* that exists at the highest levels of government (and among well-remunerated "professional" layers) about what's building up among working people in cities, towns, and countryside. It's the fear that is shaking both parties of the capitalist ruling families.

"There hasn't been nearly enough blaming of the people most responsible for [Donald Trump's] rise: his voters," writes liberal *Washington Post* columnist Charles Lane. These workers, he says, want to "blow the system to hell."

Venting in the stronghold of the conservative wing of this anti-working-class alliance, *National Review* writer Kevin Williamson more explicitly and crudely denounces "white working class dysfunction." These "downscale communities . . . deserve to die," he says. "Economically they are negative assets. Morally, they are indefensible. . . . The white American underclass is in thrall to a vicious, selfish culture whose main products are misery and used heroin needles. Donald Trump's speeches make them feel good. So does OxyContin."

We're living through the biggest crisis of the capitalist parties in the lifetime of anyone reading these pages. If anything, the disarray is greater in the Democratic Party than the Republican. The millions who've flocked to Bernie Sanders's call, resuscitating "Occupy" in bourgeois electoral garb, pose an unexpected obstacle to Hillary Clinton's anointment as the Democrats' 2016 candidate, and her election if nominated.

But what is surfacing in the 2016 presidential election is neither unexpected nor unexplainable. Its roots go back several decades. If you want to understand it, there's no better place to start than this book.

Are They Rich Because They're Smart? Class, Privilege, and Learning Under Capitalism contains three articles by Jack Barnes, National Secretary of the Socialist Workers Party, taken from talks and reports he gave to large public audiences between 1995 and 2009. More recent statistics and subsequent events that shed light on the economic and social contradictions fueling today's political upheaval have been taken into account by incorporating them directly into the text. This spares readers from the distraction of frequent footnotes and parenthetical material. The original articles are available in the books indicated in accompanying source notes.

The growing disorder of the world capitalist system has unfolded with jumps and starts over the past forty years—since the 1974–75 global recession, Vietnam War–fueled inflation surges, and "energy" crises of that time. Those shocks laid the groundwork for the 1987 Wall Street crash, which—like jittery animals sensing a coming earthquake—foretold the cumulative effects of the capitalists' falling profit rates and contraction of rate of investment in capacity-expanding plant, equipment, and employment.

In an attempt to postpone a shattering collapse, the US ruling families and their rivals resorted to a renewed debt spree—this time worldwide, and even more mammoth than the lending bonanza of the 1980s. They've fought tenaciously to press wages down, enlarge the reserve army of unemployed labor, intensify speedup on the job at the cost of life and limb, and make further progress in weakening the unions. They've done everything in their power to foster competition and conflict among workers. The employers' hope is to create the conditions necessary to induce a new wave of capital accumulation and sustained expansion of production and trade before confronting a rising challenge by the working class and labor movement to their inhuman system of exploitation.

This book comes off the presses during the eighth year of what Washington logs as an "economic recovery." For working people in the US, from big cities to farming areas, that "upturn" has been marked by rising rents and home foreclosures, a *fall* in median household income, and historic lows in the percentage of workers actually holding a job (the government's headline unemployment figures notwithstanding).

Interest rates are at their lowest levels in the history of the imperialist world. Short-term rates have scraped zero year after year in the United States, and in parts of capitalist Europe and Japan interest rates have been pushed into negative territory—a tax on the bourgeoisie imposed by money capital with the will-o'-the-wisp goal of somehow facilitating growth. For the working class and lower middle classes, *both* zero and negative rates are a ruinous tax on those who depend on a pension or "savings" account for help to get by.

In short, capitalism is well into a slow-burning global depression.

What's more, the US rulers have engaged in nonstop wars and military operations since the turn of the millennium (not to mention the bloody 1991 Gulf War and the first war on European soil since World War II in the former Yugoslavia during the administrations of George H.W. Bush and Bill Clinton). Just since September 11, 2001, the presidencies of Republican George W. Bush and Democrat Barack Obama have fought wars or carried out airstrikes, shelling, drone assaults, and Special Forces operations in Iraq, Afghanistan, Pakistan, Libya, Yemen, Syria, and elsewhere.

Hundreds of thousands of workers and peasants in these countries have been killed or maimed by all sides in military conflicts since 2001, and millions left homeless, hungry, and dispossessed. Nearly 7,000 US soldiers have died and more than 52,000 have been wounded—disproportionately young men and women from rural areas and urban working-class neighborhoods, who've faced scandalous neglect on return.

All the above are among the reasons so many working people are coming out to listen to and vote for Donald Trump. And they explain large elements of why other workers, even if smaller in number, give a hearing to Bernie Sanders, as well.

Contrary to the drumbeat in the corporate media, this crisis in the capitalist parties has nothing to do with a nonexistent rise of racism within a nonexistent "white working class." There's *a working class* in the United States. Among other things, these workers are Black, Latino, Asian, African, and (for now and decades to come) a majority are Caucasian. More and more are of mixed race as well. Racism and racist acts have been *pushed back* as a result of the conquests of the mass, proletarian-based struggle for Black rights, including among the growing numbers of working men and women of various skin colors, mother tongues, and national origins who work together side by side in factories and other workplaces day in and day out.

"I have never voted, and I'm not here to represent the Republican Party. Quite frankly, I don't give a damn about the Republicans," said former basketball coach Bobby Knight to tumultuous cheers as he introduced Trump to some twelve thousand participants in an April 28 rally in Evansville, Indiana. "I don't give a damn about the Democrats either."

At least on these double "don't give a damns," Knight echoed the sentiments of growing millions in the working class and worse-off middle classes across the United States.

◆

Are They Rich Because They're Smart? puts a spotlight on the sharpening class inequalities in the United States, especially the relatively recent and accelerated expansion of a high-earning professional and upper middle-class layer in US capitalist society.

This "self-designated 'enlightened meritocracy'"—of millions, if not tens of millions, the author says—is composed overwhelmingly of those pursuing "careers in the universities, the media, 'think tanks,' [as well as] highly paid supervisory personnel, staffers, or attorneys [for] foundations, 'advocacy groups,' NGOs, charities, and other 'nonprofit' institutions."

They are determined "to con the world into accepting the myth that the economic and social advancement of its members is just reward for their individual intelligence, education, and 'service.' Its members truly believe that their 'brightness,' their 'quickness,' their 'contributions to public life' . . . give them the right to make decisions, to administer and 'regulate' society for the bourgeoisie—on behalf of what they claim to be the interests of 'the people,'" an imaginary and classless "we."

Just during the week this book was being readied for the presses, two articles—one in the liberal *Washington Post*, the other in the conservative *Wall Street Journal*—captured to a "T" the spoken or unspoken class attitudes of many in this meritocratic layer.

"Never have so many people with so little knowledge made so many consequential decisions for the rest of us," wrote David Harsanyi in a May 20 *Post* column headlined, "We must weed out ignorant Americans from the electorate."

Then, two days later in the *Journal*, Andy Kessler wrote, "Hollywood movies notwithstanding, capitalism is not about greed. It is a system that weeds out dumb ideas from smart ones." It would have been impolitic for Kessler to come right out and say it's a system that "weeds out dumb *people* from smart *people*," but people both "dumb" and "smart" are able to read.

As Barnes points out, this social layer has a special place in overseeing one of the shifts that marks the evolution of the US imperialist state since the closing decades of the twentieth century: the centralization of powers initially reserved in the US Constitution to the legislative branch of government (the House of Representatives and Senate, and their counterparts on the state level) in a more and more dominant executive branch (the White House and its multiplying "regulatory" agencies and "administrators").

There's no way for the working class to vote or legislate itself to power, or to the revolutionary expropriation of the propertied ruling families and the transition to socialism. But the expanding concentration of power in the hands of the presidency—including the de facto power to declare wars, and to bypass legislation and debate by issuing Executive Orders—is dangerous (ultimately a bonapartist threat) to the interests of workers, working farmers, and the labor movement.

Today there is even an Office of Information and Regulatory Affairs in the White House, established by Executive Order in 1993 during the Clinton administration. The agency's director during Obama's first term, Cass Sunstein, coined a term for this aspiration of middle-class meritocrats to administer and regulate the lives of the unwashed masses, who can't be trusted to know what's in our own interests. He christened it with a book titled *Nudge: Improving Decisions about Health, Wealth, and Happiness* (that is, getting us to do what they think is "best for us," without us having a say or figuring out they're trying to manipulate us).

The actual scope of the expansion of the imperialist state is much greater and more invasive in the lives of working people than just "nudges," of course. According to Washington's own figures, there are some 510 federal departments and agencies today, none of which are elected and whose decision making is never seen on CSPAN or anywhere else.

What's more, under cover of "national security" and "fighting terrorism" (and now vastly aided by "social media" technologies), the tentacles of police surveillance at the federal, state, and local levels have increasingly penetrated every aspect of our lives and eroded hard-won rights that protect us *against* the state. This massive snooping has become an emblem—a *hated* emblem—of imperialist America the world over.

◆

There is as yet no rising working-class social movement in the United States in response to assaults on our wages, living conditions, and political rights. But over the past few years there have been strikes and resistance to lockouts by members of the United Steelworkers, Communications Workers of America, Teamsters, farmworkers organizations, and other unions. Fast-food and other low-paid workers are demanding a $15 hourly minimum wage.

Tens of thousands have come into the streets to protest police killings and brutality and demand the arrest and prosecution of the cops responsible. Workers and their families are raising their voices against the massive penal system in the US, with its draconian sentences, brutalizing solitary confinement, and official barbarities. Immigrant workers and their supporters have organized to speak out against deportations, E-Verify victimizations, and other indignities. Mounting attacks on a woman's right to choose abortion continue to be met with protests.

Above all, there is growing confidence and openness among workers everywhere in the United States to discuss and debate the broadest social and political questions, including the stakes for the working class in organizing the unorganized and rebuilding our unions as instruments of solidarity and struggle.

These political opportunities are not an impression from outside the working class. They're the practical conclusion from half a decade of efforts by members and supporters of the Socialist Workers Party going door to door in working-class neighborhoods of all kinds across the country to talk with and exchange experiences and views with fellow workers.

The heart of these discussions—whether on a porch, at an apartment door, at a strike picket or social protest, or life on the job—is never simply about "issues," even political questions of great importance to the working class. It's about the way forward. It's about what Jack Barnes points to in the closing article in this book as "preparing the working class for the greatest of all battles in the years ahead— the battle to throw off the self-image the rulers teach us, and to recognize that we are capable of taking power and organizing society."

That's the conclusion that's decisive for workers everywhere today. To act on the necessity, as we gain confidence and experience fighting alongside each other, for the working class to recognize our humanity, our capacities, and the traditions our class has forged during well over a century and half of struggles, including revolutionary battles and victories. "To broaden our scope," to discover our "own worth," as Malcolm X was always explaining.

"Learning as a lifetime experience," as the author puts it in these pages—what better reason to make a socialist revolution? "What better reason to get rid of the capitalist state and use the workers state to begin transforming humanity, to begin building human solidarity? And we have the living example of the Cuban Revolution to show how it's possible to start down that road."

These are the stakes addressed in *Are They Rich Because They're Smart? Class, Privilege, and Learning Under Capitalism.*

Steve Clark
MAY 30, 2016

Are they rich because they're smart? The rationalization of class privilege

"The scandal of *The Bell Curve* in bourgeois public opinion is its open defense of class inequality and privilege. It's a rationalization for the bipartisan convergence around anti-working-class economic and social policy."

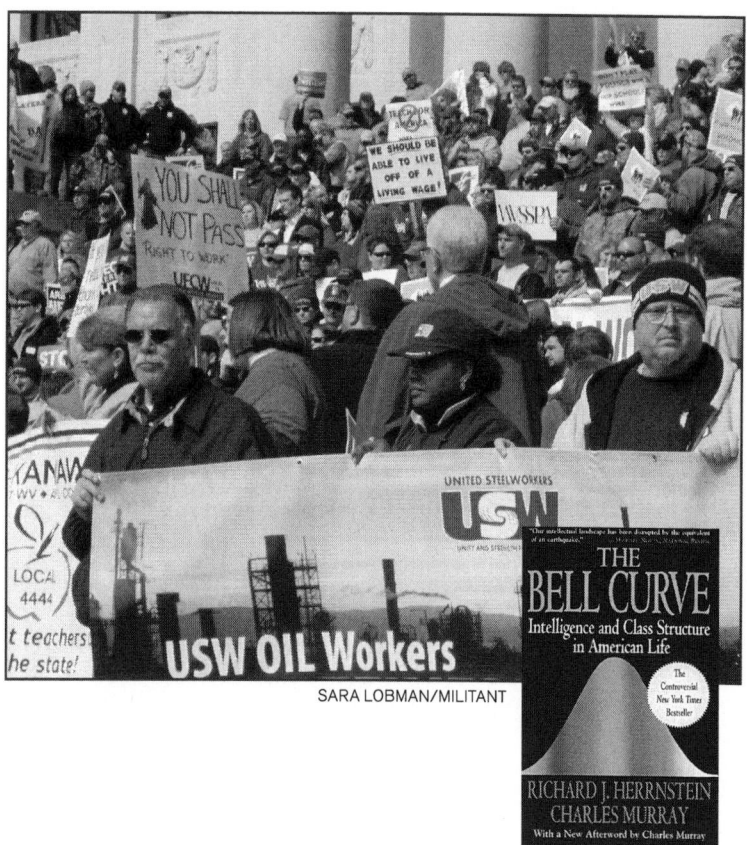

SARA LOBMAN/MILITANT

"Some in the ruling class are beginning to see what's coming as they press harder and harder against workers. They know the working class too can be pushed to be mean as well as lean."

Above: Union-organized rally at state capitol in Charleston, West Virginia, March 2015, protesting unsafe working conditions, antiunion legislation, cuts to school funding, and low wages. In front row, refinery workers on strike against Marathon Oil in Catlettsburg, Kentucky.

Are they rich because they're smart? The rationalization of class privilege

DAVID ROSENFELD: You had some things to say earlier today about Yale economists. I wonder what your opinion is of the Harvard professors who came up with the recently published book *The Bell Curve*. I'm especially interested in why *The Bell Curve* has made such a splash in the media. Why it is that every decade or so, it seems, this theory of genetically determined intellectual superiority or racial superiority gets regurgitated and debated and debunked, and then comes back in another form? And in *The Bell Curve*, the form isn't even that different from the past. So why does it seem to have such staying power?[1]

This exchange took place during the discussion period after a December 31, 1994, talk by Jack Barnes to a socialist educational conference in Los Angeles, California, cosponsored by the Socialist Workers Party and the Young Socialists. A report by Barnes based on the opening and closing talks at that weekend regional conference was discussed and adopted by delegates to the SWP's 38th National Convention, held July 8–12, 1995, in Oberlin, Ohio. The talk, entitled "So Far from God, So Close to Orange County: The Deflationary Drag of Finance Capital," was published in the collection *Capitalism's World Disorder* (Pathfinder, 1999).

JACK BARNES: If my memory serves me right, only one of the authors—Richard Herrnstein—was a Harvard professor; he died shortly before the book was released in September. Murray, a Harvard graduate, is currently hired by one of the Republican think tanks in Washington, DC, the American Enterprise Institute.

I've read about four hundred fifty pages of *The Bell Curve*, including the last two chapters, which are the most important. I don't intend to read any more—and, yes, there's a lot more.

The recurring debate you referred to is over a political matter, not a scientific one. The debate is not about the bell curve, neither the statistical concept nor this new book by that name. What's at issue is the attempt to defend the wealth and class privilege of a so-called meritocratic social layer—"the cognitive elite" is the euphemism chosen by Murray and Herrnstein.

I expected a question about the book might come up in the discussion here, so I brought my copy with me. Let me read you the first few sentences from the second-to-last chapter, entitled "The Way We Are Headed."

"In this penultimate chapter"—Herrnstein and Murray could have written "second-to-last," but they had to justify their parents having spent tens of thousands of dollars to send them to Harvard—"In this penultimate chapter we speculate about the impact of cognitive stratification on American life and government. Predicting the course of society is chancy, but certain tendencies seem strong

---

1. Richard Herrnstein and Charles Murray, *The Bell Curve: Intelligence and Class Structure in American Life* (New York: The Free Press, 1994).

enough to worry about."

"Worry about"—that's interesting language in what is supposed to be a scientific study. Then they go on to list these "worrying" tendencies:

"An increasingly isolated cognitive elite.

"A merging of the cognitive elite with the affluent.

"A deteriorating quality of life for people at the bottom end of the cognitive ability distribution."

"What's at issue in *The Bell Curve* is an attempt to defend the wealth and class privilege of a so-called meritocratic social layer—'the cognitive elite' is the euphemism chosen by the authors. . . . It's even more about social class than race."

So, that's the opening paragraph of the penultimate chapter. Now let's say it another way:

We're rich, mostly newly rich. We got rich because we're smart. You can tell we're smart because we're rich. Because we're smart and rich, our kids are smart, and are going to be rich too. But there are a lot of people who aren't getting rich, and they can't seem to accept the fact that this is simply because their forebears were dumb. The liberals—those who are rich and those who aren't—know this and live by it, but are embarrassed to say so. Most people, however, mistakenly think there is some connection between what us smart people are doing to get rich and their own deteriorating quality of life. We're getting more isolated in that sense, and a little nervous about anyone wanting to take our privileges away. But we want to enjoy being rich. There's nothing to feel guilty about. We're rich because we're smart.

That's about the long and the short of it.

Then the book ends up with some proposals about what to do with all of us "at the bottom end of the cognitive ability distribution." If we can "face reality about the underclass," the book says, then we can provide "the opportunity for everyone, not just the lucky ones, to live a satisfying life." That is, you can learn to accept being "dumb" (or be made to pretend that you are). And you can learn to like being poor (or be made to pretend you like it).

But this is only possible, the book says, if the capitalist government and employers get rid of all the by-products of working-class struggles the rulers have had to concede over decades that get in the way of "facing reality about the underclass." That includes the minimum wage; affirmative action; the extension of Social Security protections; welfare payments; and more funding for preschool education, child care, and public schools. ("For many people, there is nothing they can learn that will repay the cost of the teaching." That's my favorite sentence in the book.)

The book *is* a retread of discredited views, but not primarily scientific or pseudoscientific ones about IQ, genetics, and so on. It has some of that too, but that's not the main point. The book is subtitled, "Intelligence and Class Structure in American Life." *That* is what it is about. It's about *social class* above all, even more than it is about race. It's about the fear that the majority cannot be conned—and cannot be "lightly" policed—forever.

The Bell Curve is a rehash—not explicitly, or even consciously, but in fact—of views presented in the 1930s by a man named Bruno Rizzi in a book called *The Bureaucratization of the World*. Similar views began to be developed by James

Burnham in the 1940s. Burnham had been a prominent figure in the American Workers Party in the mid-1930s, and was a member of our National Committee following a fusion at the time between the AWP and the Communist League, a predecessor of the Socialist Workers Party. By the end of the decade he'd become a leader of petty-bourgeois currents in the SWP that bent to patriotic pressures and broke with communism during the buildup toward US entry into World War II. When they couldn't win the party to their views and proposed course, they split from the SWP in 1940.

Burnham carried his position to its logical conclusion in 1941 in a book called *The Managerial Revolution*. The entire world, he argued—whether US finance capital under the Democratic Party's "New Deal/War Deal," or the Nazi Reich aiming to salvage and exalt German imperialism, or the dominant social caste in the Soviet Union (the Stalinist regime's "meritocracy")—were converging toward social relations in which managerial "elites" and unelected bureaucrats governed and made all decisions in order to pacify and regiment the masses. Burnham subsequently became a founding editor and writer on William Buckley's magazine, *National Review*. Others—prominent New Dealers and so on—have presented their own variants of the "managerial revolution" as well.

All these writers do the same thing. They project their own privileged professions as a world-organizing force, and as a justification for incomes well above those of working people. And, at the same time, they resent the bourgeoisie and fear too broad a democracy.

Our movement has had decades of experience answering such views. Communist leader Leon Trotsky dealt with their political implications in 1939 and 1940, for example, in articles and letters collected in *In Defense of Marxism*. The book is published by Pathfinder. You can get a copy of the book at the literature table back there.

According to Murray and Herrnstein, capitalism achieved a wondrous thing by the opening years of the twentieth century. In the United States it happened even a bit earlier, they say. Before then wealth and social position had for centuries been passed on from one generation to the next through a rigid class structure—through aristocratic elites. Those in the ruling classes—from the kings and queens right on down—were often not very smart, notoriously slothful, and dissolute.

With capitalism, however, came "the career open to talent." Anyone, they say, from any class background or of any nationality or skin color, could now rise to positions of political power and material comfort—on the basis of merit, intelligence, hard work, and moral virtue.

But today something further is happening, as the level of capitalist technology and computerization advances, they add. The intelligence and competence required to keep modern society up and running is inevitably concentrating wealth and power, and more and more of it is ending up in the hands of a social layer of middle-class professionals, technocrats, managers, and academics—people, coincidentally, much like themselves. Herrnstein and Murray call this "the cognitive elite." (They could have used terms like "the intelligentsia"—or, with respect to its African American subcomponent, "the talented tenth"—but that would have been too blatant.) There is nothing that can, or should, be done about this. That's just the way it is, and has to be, due to modern technology.

"So what's the problem?" Herrnstein and Murray say.

"Millions of people have benefited from the changes—including us. Would we prefer less of a meritocracy? Put that way, no." But the authors continue:

> What worries us first about the emerging cognitive elite is its coalescence into a class that views American society increasingly through a lens of its own. . . .
>
> [They] are likely to have gone to the same kinds of schools, live in similar neighborhoods, go to the same kinds of theaters and restaurants, read the same magazines and newspapers, watch the same television programs, even drive the same makes of cars.

And the social and political consequences of this trend, Herrnstein and Murray say, threaten to extend beyond African Americans in the United States to what they label an "emerging white underclass." They write:

> The dry tinder for the formation of an underclass community is a large number of births to single women of low intelligence. . . . In the past, whites have not had an "underclass" as such, because the whites who might qualify have been too scattered among the working class. . . .
>
> An underclass needs a critical mass, and white America has not had one. But if the overall white illegitimacy rate is 22 percent—probably in the range of 40 percent in low-income communities—and rising fast, the question arises: At what point is critical mass reached?

This is why *The Bell Curve* has produced a bit of a scandal in bourgeois public opinion, across the political spectrum but especially among liberals. At bottom, the furor is not primarily because of what the book says about race. The scandal is its open self-rationalization of the class inequality and privilege benefiting a growing upper-middle-class layer, and its justification for the anti-working-class bipartisan convergence around economic and social policy.

Admit it, Murray and Herrnstein say to middle-class liberals, isn't this what all of us in this privileged social layer really think? Isn't it how all of us really act? Isn't this why we all live where we live? Isn't it why more and more of us send our kids to private schools? Isn't it why we hire round-the-clock private cops to patrol our gated neighborhoods? Don't feel guilty. We're rich because we deserve to be rich.

In fact, in the chapter I've been describing, Murray and Herrnstein directly say that during "the [George H.W.] Bush and [William] Clinton administrations, the old lines began to blur" between liberals and conservatives. They talk in *The Bell Curve* about the "cognitive elite" versus those who "aren't very smart." Labor secretary Robert Reich, Clinton's house liberal, talks in his book *The Work of Nations* about the "symbolic analysts" at the top of the income ladder versus the "in-person servers" and "routine producers" who comprise the majority of the population.

This is also why a layer of rightists in bourgeois politics like Patrick Buchanan have given thumbs down to *The Bell Curve* (and to *The Work of Nations*). Murray and Herrnstein and Reich glorify the "elites" who the rightists rail against. "I think America is a land of opportunity where B students and C students have had A students working for them for generations," Buchanan said in response to *The Bell Curve*. "In America it is not IQ that is destiny; it is character, courage, ambition, drive, personality, all of these things."

That is the kind of demagogy Buchanan aims at sections of the middle class, and receptive and disoriented layers of the working class, who are under growing economic pressure as a result of capitalism's deflationary squeeze. But it's closer to reality, and closer to the gut reactions of millions, than *The Bell Curve*, so Buchanan gets a wider hearing than Charles Murray and Richard Hernnstein.

Mounting bourgeois concerns

But the scandal around *The Bell Curve* is just one small reflection of concerns voiced by some in the bourgeoisie about the potentially explosive consequences of what is happening in the world capitalist economy, including the effects of the employers' "successes" in downsizing and cost cutting. Some of them are taking a look at what is building up among the working classes in the United States and other parts of the world, and it is beginning to scare them. It is not just communists who can see developments ultimately heading toward intensified class struggle.

A couple of weeks ago, the former editor of the *New York Times*, A.M. Rosenthal, entitled one of his regular op-ed page columns "Lean and Very Mean." He ended with this paragraph:

> If leanness-meanness goes on too long and American optimism finally dies, workers may one day fill the streets again. There will be no F.D.R. to rescue capitalism. . . . American business will find out how very mean life can get.

A.M. Rosenthal is not what they used to call a "bleeding-heart liberal." He is a social conservative, who has been praising big business for being lean and mean for a decade or more. But this is the unexpected outcome he now fears. (By the way, Rosenthal still uses the initials "A.M.," because when he started with the *New York Times* during World War II, if you were Jewish and had a name like Abraham, you weren't allowed to use it on articles or columns and had to go by your initials. The capitalist family that owns the *Times* is Jewish, and that was one of the ways they accommodated to their niche in the US ruling class, where anti-Semitism is the rule, not the exception. Rosenthal has reason to be slightly more concerned than some others in the "isolated cognitive elite.")

About a month earlier, there was an opinion column in the London business daily, the *Financial Times*. The column is called the "Global Investor," and the headline last November 14 was "Work Harder, or Not at All." Think about that for a while—"Work Harder, or Not at All." I'm not making it up.

The column is accompanied by a chart, with three lines tracing indexes bourgeois commentators (and "economists") use to measure productivity in the United States. One line is labeled "manufacturing output"—with a couple of dips, it goes up since 1991. The second line is labeled "hours worked"—it goes up too. Then there is the third line, labeled "compensation per hour"—it slides down. There is nothing like a chart to belatedly confirm what every working person already knows and has felt in our bones!

The columnist opens by pointing out that over the previous three months in the United States, profits were "up strongly," sales were "also up sharply," and "many manufacturers said they were still shedding labour." And then he adds: "Here is productivity and no mistake. If this is what the peak of the cycle looks like, God help the workers in the next downturn." [Alas, there has been no such divine assistance to the working class over the two decades since 1995, as shown by the graphs on page 33.—JB]

That's what's catching the attention of many spokespersons for the bourgeoisie—including the "scientists" who wrote *The Bell Curve*. Yes, we want to push profits up. Yes, we want to be wealthy. Yes, that means we have to keep wages down, push hours up, and speed up production. But isn't this all leading toward a reaction by workers? The *Financial Times* article even mentions *The Bell Curve*, commenting that "one does not have to accept the argument to take the point: one way or another, the technological revolution is social dynamite." Leave aside the foolishness that it is "technological revolution"—not the effects of the bosses' cost cutting and downsizing, the effects of the social relations of capitalism—that is "social dynamite." But the *Financial Times* columnist does get the political point.

While we're at it, Rosenthal gives a little too much credit to the power of New York bourgeois aristocrats in stating that "F.D.R. saved capitalism" during the depression of the 1930s. Once workers are engaged in concerted struggle, few of them, especially class-conscious workers, listen to much of anything most capitalist politicians have to say, including Franklin Roosevelt. What Rosenthal leaves out of the story of the 1930s are the AFL and CIO union bureaucracy, the Communist Party, and the Socialist Party and other social democratic and centrist misleaderships. These are the class-collaborationist forces who—from within the workers organizations, under the growing pressure of social-patriotic war mongering—derailed the social power of the rising industrial union movement by diverting it into support for the capitalist two-party system.

It's not only thinking workers who can see what is building up under today's deflationary conditions. If what we see happening all around us—declining real wages, longer hours, deteriorating safety conditions, growing impoverishment—is what is happening in the third year of an *expansion* in the business cycle, then what is in store with the next not-so-soft landing? And what kind of struggles by workers will that lead to when the cycle turns up a little bit and there is more room to resist?

Politics, not science

These are the real questions to keep in mind when we are discussing *The Bell Curve*. There are undoubtedly many legitimate criticisms that can be, and have been, made about the book's genetics, its reading or misreading of various studies, its statistical methods, and so on. To cite just one example, average IQ levels both in the industrially advanced countries and many parts of the semicolonial world have gone up substantially since World War II. But if that's what the figures show, and it is (as cited even by Murray and Herrnstein), then this cannot possibly be the product of genetic shifts; it cannot have anything to do with evolution. It is much too short a time.

These figures reflect changes in social relations, in productive human beings' concept of ourselves, in how we spend our time, in what we do and how we act. They register the growth in the size of the working class. They register the continuing racial integration of the working class in all areas of work. They register the drawing of more women out of the home into the labor force. They register the growing numbers of toilers who have access to primary education

"There is nothing like a chart to belatedly confirm what every working person already knows and has felt in our bones!"

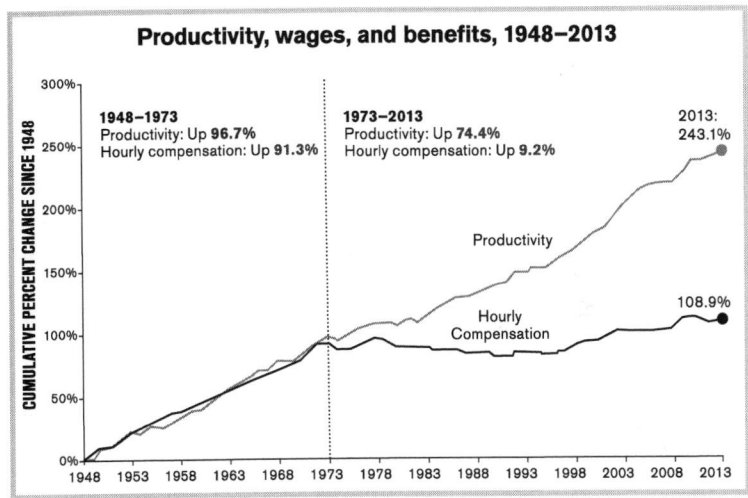

Compensation figures are inflation-adjusted wages for nonsupervisory production workers. Economic Policy Institute

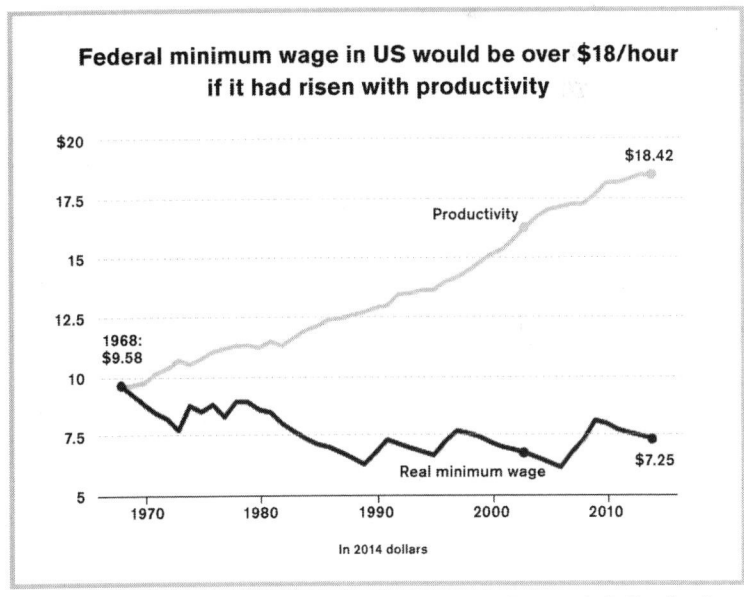

Economic Policy Institute

"In the 1930s the union bureaucracy, the Communist Party, Socialist Party, and other class-collaborationist forces within the workers organizations derailed the power of the industrial union movement by diverting it into support for the capitalist system."

Above: Sit-down strike paralyzed General Motors in Flint, Michigan, January 1937, forcing bosses to recognize United Auto Workers union. **Inset:** As industrial unions advanced, so did confidence among workers that they could break with capitalism's twin parties and form a labor party based on the unions. Stalinists, Socialist Party leaders, and some labor bureaucrats formed American Labor Party to head off such a course and corral support for Roosevelt from workers who might refuse to vote "Democrat."

and improved nutrition, as well as other social factors.

But good science or bad is not primarily what is involved with *The Bell Curve*. Neither Richard Herrnstein nor Charles Murray are geneticists. Murray is a political propagandist, who got a big name during the Reagan administration for writing a book saying the government should get rid of welfare programs—a book called *Losing Ground: American Social Policy 1950–1980*. The Reagan administration praised the book but was not about to follow its advice. Reagan cut some taxes for the rich and that was about it. The Reagan White House actually increased federal spending across the board, including for welfare payments. It took Clinton, who said publicly on TV that Murray's writings on the social effects of Aid to Families with Dependent Children were "essentially right," to begin pushing the need for legislation to abolish "welfare as we know it."

Murray says, yes, we have to get rid of welfare. That is the necessary first step toward slashing government-funded social programs that eat into profits. Get rid of welfare and let the chips fall where they may. That is the only way "we" are ever going to get to the point where "we" will be able to walk around safely again in our cities, he says.

Nobody in the ruling class has, or can have, any solution to the crisis of the capitalist system, and none of them, of course, has any alternative to doing what is necessary to maximize profits. What could they propose? To stop competing? To raise wages and cut hours, while their rivals are cutting wages and extending hours? To stop using cops as a feared control force?

But more of them are beginning to see what is coming as the decline accelerates and as they press harder and harder against the working class. Some are old enough to

"Nobody in the ruling class has any solution to the capitalist crisis. What could they do? Stop competing? Raise wages while their rivals cut wages? Stop using cops and prisons as a feared control force?"

LUCAS JACKSON/REUTERS

MARVIN JACKSON

Top: Outpouring in Baltimore, Maryland, May 2015, protesting killing of Freddie Gray, whose neck was broken while shackled in a police van.

Below: Striking Verizon workers shout at strikebreakers, escorted by police, at call center in Garden City, NY, May 2016. 39,000 unionists walked out over bosses' drive to boost profits by reducing labor costs.

remember earlier periods in the history of capitalism, or have read enough about them, to know what happens when growing labor battles and other social struggles start overlapping and interconnecting. They know that the employers find out that the working class too can be pushed to be mean as well as lean.

"Human beings have a genetic structure and variability. But we're not computers. Not only our hardware but our software begins changing as soon as we start doing things with our hands and eyes when we're still infants. Social practice and experience make us what we are."

The hype around *The Bell Curve* has already peaked, but workers' resistance to what the capitalists are trying to impose will not go away. Nor will their growing—and destabilizing—skepticism about the wisdom and permanence of the Democratic and Republican parties.

Most of the debate around *The Bell Curve* in the bourgeois press was never serious. Most did not amount to much more than scolding the authors that no matter what they think about these questions, *they just shouldn't say it.* Now is not the time. It's too explosive.

There is no basis in bourgeois politics right now for some new rise of a reactionary eugenics movement. There was nothing scientific about the Nazis' racial theories. They couldn't come into their own until the working class had been defeated and fascism had triumphed in Germany. That was a political, not a scientific question. (And we should re-

"The concept of race, in its virulent and pseudoscientific forms—as a justification for chattel slavery, for example—is a product of the rise of industrial capitalism."

"There was nothing scientific about the Nazis' racial theories. They couldn't come into their own until the working class had been defeated and fascism had triumphed in Germany. That was a political, not a scientific question."

Top: Slave auctions, Louisiana, 1842; South Carolina, 1769.

Bottom: Buchenwald, one of the largest concentration camps within Nazi Germany, where more than 50,000 Jews and others were murdered.

call that before Nazism gave eugenics a bad name, many of its biggest boosters in the early 1900s were liberal, social democratic, and anarchist meritocrats of their day. These included Sidney and Beatrice Webb, John Maynard Keynes, Margaret Sanger, Havelock Ellis, H.G. Wells, W.E.B. Du Bois, George Bernard Shaw, Bertrand Russell, Peter Kropotkin, and Emma Goldman.)

Anyway, *The Bell Curve* says it's the Jews and Japanese who are the really smart ones, not the Aryans. So that nixes its appeal straight away with the "America Firsters" and white supremacists. They aren't interested in any eugenics program that could end up phasing out white folks and putting Jews and Asians on top! Hell no, we won't go! If that's the choice, they prefer Patrick Buchanan to Murray and Herrnstein—you can bet on that.

Human beings, of course, have a genetic structure and variability. But we are not computers. It is not just our hardware that changes. Our software changes, too. It changes as soon as we start doing things with our hands and eyes when we're still just tiny infants. Social practice and experience make us what we are. There are also some things about human beings, of course, that do not change, no matter what happens to us socially. We come in different sexes. We have different skin pigmentation. We have certain different health disorders and reactions to medical treatments. And there are many other examples. The world would be awfully boring if this weren't true.

But none of this is reducible to some built-in limit to the potential of human beings, or of any socially defined group of human beings. Because both classes and races *are* historically determined products of the rise of class-divided society. The concept of race, in its virulent and pseudoscientific forms—as a justification for chattel slavery, for example—is the product of only the most recent stage in class society. It is both a precondition of what Karl Marx called "the primitive accumulation of capital," and a consequence of the rise and consolidation of modern industrial capitalism.

"The struggle for workers power, and the transformation of property relations necessary to open the transition to socialism, are possible only as working people begin transforming ourselves and our attitudes toward life, work, and each other. Only then will we learn what we're capable of becoming."

All the great Marxists have gloried in how the building of socialism will enable working people to transform ourselves—to transform who we are and what we are capable of. Read the *Communist Manifesto* and other writings by Karl Marx and Frederick Engels. Read what V.I. Lenin, Leon Trotsky, and other Bolshevik leaders had to say about this. Read the articles and books by James P. Cannon and Farrell Dobbs. Read the books by George Novack and by Evelyn Reed recounting humanity's millennia-long ascent. Read Malcolm X. Read Fidel Castro. Read *Socialism and Man in Cuba* and other works by Ernesto Che Guevara. Read Maurice Bishop and Thomas Sankara.

It is social labor that makes possible all civilization and the advance of culture. Working people begin to transform ourselves and strengthen bonds of human solidarity in the very process of building the fighting social movements and disciplined proletarian organizations without which the capitalist rulers will plunge the world into fascism and war.

The revolutionary struggle for workers power—and even more, the fundamental transformation of property relations necessary to open the transition to socialism—is possible only through the organization of working people to begin transforming ourselves and our attitudes toward life and work and each other. Only then will we learn what we're capable of becoming, as we unfold the capacities of ourselves and our allies to change society.

What the social labor of human beings will make possible under communism will put humanity so far above the shoulders of those whom we today consider the great thinkers and doers of history that we cannot even conceive the terms of comparison.

Growing class stratification
and the 'enlightened meritocracy'

"The Congressional Black Caucus members weren't honoring Clinton for promoting economic and social advancement of the toiling majority of African Americans or workers and farmers as a whole. They were honoring him for his contribution to their own career advancement and that of their peers."

Above: Bill and Hillary Clinton at September 1999 Congressional Black Caucus awards dinner. Two years later the annual banquet named him "America's first Black president."

Growing class stratification and the 'enlightened meritocracy'

THE TONGUE-IN-CHEEK anointment of William Jefferson Clinton as "the first Black president" of the United States during a Congressional Black Caucus awards dinner in late 2001 was more than simply a post-cocktails laugh line. It registered the consolidation of a bourgeoisified social layer of African Americans, a by-product of the increasing class stratification of the Black population and an inevitable capitalist perversion of victories won by the Black rights movement of the 1950s and 1960s. This process was reinforced by the credit-fueled capitalist "prosperity" and "good times" of much of the 1990s that began unraveling during the opening decade of the twenty-first century.

Within the Black nationality there had been a signifi-

Based on reports by Jack Barnes to an April 11–13, 2009, Socialist Workers Party leadership conference in New York and a November 22, 2008, talk to a meeting of some 375 participants held in Newark, New Jersey, sponsored by the SWP and the Young Socialists. An earlier version, entitled "The Cosmopolitan 'Meritocracy' and the Changing Class Structure of the Black Nationality," appeared in *Malcolm X, Black Liberation, and the Road to Workers Power* (Pathfinder, 2009). Many facts and figures have been updated as of May 2016.

cant growth of middle-class and professional layers, even a bourgeois layer—to a degree unthinkable to people of all classes and races in the United States no more than a quarter century earlier. Well before his term in the White House began in 1993, Clinton had recognized the usefulness of this development for the stability of capitalist rule in the United States, and in particular its importance for the Democratic Party at the local, state, and federal levels. Clinton appointed many more Blacks to his administration than did any of the forty-one presidents before him, or, so far, the two after him. He named nine African Americans to cabinet-level positions and nine as assistants to the president, not to mention thousands of appointments to other posts throughout the federal bureaucracy.

The Black Caucus members were not honoring Clinton for promoting the economic and social advancement of the toiling majority of African Americans or of workers and farmers as a whole in the United States. They were honoring him for his contribution to their own career advancement and that of their social peers.

This fact was underlined some fifteen years later when the Congressional Black Caucus Political Action Committee, early in the primary cycle, announced its endorsement of Hillary Clinton for the 2016 presidential nomination. New York congressman Gregory Meeks, chair of CBC PAC, praised Clinton—in reality referring more to her husband Bill than to the candidate herself—for helping Congressional Black Caucus members become chairs of subcommittees and for being "on the stump with us" over the years.

It's important for the working-class movement to understand the scope and pace of the expansion of this upper middle-class layer of the Black population, which has existed for a generation or two at most, as well as its limits. This is different from the small middle class among African Americans throughout most of the twentieth century: school teachers; preachers at large churches; owners of funeral parlors, auto dealerships, and other small businesses catering to Blacks; and a handful of lawyers, accountants, and doctors practicing almost exclusively in Black neighborhoods and serving Black-owned businesses.

One indication of the newness of this middle class within the African American nationality is the lag between the growth in its members' median annual *income*—which expanded quite rapidly once certain racist barriers were battered down by the Black rights movement—and their median *wealth*. Unlike income, wealth (often called a person's "net worth" [!] under capitalism) takes a lot longer to accumulate and to pass along tax free through inheritance and family trusts and foundations.

While the median household *income* of Blacks was nearly 60 percent of that of Caucasians in 2014, the median family *wealth* of Black families was just over 6 percent that of whites. What's more, that wealth gap has widened since the 2007–08 crisis hit, and a much higher percentage of the wealth held by Blacks is accounted for by a house, not by stocks, bonds, and other capital. In that sense, Blacks remain "house rich and cash poor," as the old expression goes. (For the tiny handful of propertied ruling families, bonds—government, agency, and corporate—are the single biggest storehouse of the "permanent" wealth they obtain from their share in the total surplus value squeezed from exploiting the social labor of workers, farmers, and other toiling producers around the world.)

This well-off social layer of the African American population also has substantially more weight than ever before among Democratic Party officeholders and functionaries. By the closing two years of the Obama administration, forty-six members of the US House of Representatives were Black—more than 10 percent—up from four members, or less than 1 percent, in 1963. As of 2010, the number of state legislators who are African American (roughly 9 percent) had tripled since 1970, and nearly a third were elected in districts with predominantly white populations. Blacks are mayors of some fifty of the six hundred US cities with populations of fifty thousand or more, while prior to 1967 there had not been a single African American mayor of a major city since the bloody crushing of Radical Reconstruction almost a century earlier.

In fact, this social layer of the Black population has become the third leg of the "coalition" that turns out the vote for the ruling-class families who run the Democratic Party—the other two being the trade union officialdom and the patronage-based political machines of major US cities. The political representatives of this layer have replaced the "Dixiecrats," the Democratic Party functionaries of the former Confederate states, who prior to the defeat of Jim Crow segregation in the 1960s had for decades formed the institutional bulwark of that racist system and guaranteed the Democrats' viability as a national party.

The meritocracy: Not 'a Black thing'

This growth of the Black middle classes and newly enlarged Black bourgeoisie is a shift that was already largely behind us when Barack Obama was elected in 2008. In fact, it culminated *politically* during the Clinton administration of 1993 to 2000.

Despite what is often said in the capitalist media and elsewhere, Obama's election as president registers not only the existence of this social layer among African Americans but something broader in the evolution of class relations in the United States. For the big majority of those who voted for Obama in 2008 and again in 2012, it's not "a Black thing."

"Obama's election registers not only the expansion of an upper middle-class layer among African Americans but a broader evolution of class relations. It's not 'a Black thing.' It's the explosive growth of a new stratum of bourgeois-minded professionals and other middle-class individuals— of all colors and hues."

The Obama administration owes its ascension to the explosive growth over the past few decades of a new stratum of bourgeois-minded professionals and middle-class individuals—*of all colors and hues*—in cities, suburbs, and university towns across the country.

From the beginning of Bill Clinton's years in Arkansas state politics in the mid-1970s, he had opportunistically recognized what the by-products of the conquests of the Black rights struggle opened for Democratic Party politicians such as himself. From the outset Clinton actively *worked* to ensure himself and his party a broader and broader "Black vote."

The Obama phenomenon came later and is quite different. Not only did Obama not need to exert a big effort during his election campaign to win the vote of the overwhelming majority of African Americans (96 percent in 2008, and 93 percent four years later), there is virtually nothing he could realistically have done *to lose it*. Obama also won some two-thirds of the votes of Latinos and student youth, including a sizable majority of students who are Caucasian. And leaving aside how bourgeois pollsters and others define "white workers," Obama got 40 percent and 36 percent of their votes in 2008 and 2012 respectively, as well.

For these reasons, while Clinton's relationship with the Congressional Black Caucus and bourgeois misleaders of civil rights, labor, and women's organizations was to some degree symbiotic, he certainly needed these "brothers and sisters" as much, if not more, than they needed him. But Barack Obama's relationship with the Black Caucus and other misleaderships is decidedly *not* symbiotic; *they* need *him*, not vice versa.

This expanding layer of the comfortable middle classes I'm talking about is composed of the handsomely remunerated staffs of so-called nonprofit foundations, charities, "community organizations," and "nongovernmental organizations" (NGOs) in the United States; of well-placed professors and top university administrative personnel; of attorneys, lobbyists, media and sports "personalities," and others. The lives and livelihoods of these growing foundation- and university-centered strata in capitalist society—who, along with bankers and businessmen, cycle back and forth into and out of government positions—are themselves largely unconnected to the production, reproduction, or circulation of social wealth. Their existence is more and more alien to the conditions of life of working people or other producers of *any* racial or national background.

This reality was reflected in the 2008 presidential election results. It wasn't the so-called Black vote that pushed

Obama so decisively over the top in the race against Republican John McCain. Among the most striking changes from previous elections is that Obama won 52 percent of the votes from those with annual incomes of more than $200,000, whereas Democrat John Kerry had barely won 35 percent of this layer only four years earlier.

"This aspiring social layer is bourgeois in its class interests, values, and world outlook—in who it serves. But it's not a section of the capitalist class in becoming. It's not 'entrepreneurial.' ... They skim off a portion of surplus value produced by working people and appropriated by the bourgeoisie. Yet most of them contribute nothing to the creation of that value."

And for the first time in many decades, the Democratic presidential candidate in 2008 won more than 50% of the votes in the nation's largely Caucasian suburbs, compared to the 41% and 47% share taken by Clinton in 1992 and 1996. What's more, while the Republicans still dominated many suburbs populated by more established "old wealth"—places such as New Canaan and Darien, Connecticut; Saddle River and Englewood Cliffs, New Jersey; or Sunfish Lake and North Oaks, Minnesota—he tallied substantial margins in towns with larger congregations of high-income professionals—places such as Westport (65%), West Hartford (70%), and Greenwich (54%), Connecticut; Montclair (84%), Tenafly (64%), and Ridgewood (56%), New Jersey; Edina (56%), Minnesota; and numerous others. More than 65% of voters in Scarsdale, one of New York City's most exclusive suburbs, voted for Obama, and Westchester County—the second wealthiest county in the state, and twelfth richest in the United States—went for Obama by a 63% margin (up from 58% for Kerry in 2004 and 56% for Clinton in 1996).

The aspiring social layer the president is part of is *bourgeois* in its class interests, its values, its world outlook—in who it serves. But it's not a section of the capitalist class in becoming. It's not "entrepreneurial," aside from a handful of technology and "social media" billionaires. It's not composed of the owners, top managers, or large debt holders of rapidly expanding new businesses—factories, farms, or financial or commercial enterprises.

The long, debt-fueled capitalist "boom" that shattered in 2007–08 was marked by the drying up of investment in capacity-expanding plant and equipment, and by an accompanying slowness in the drawing of production labor into the creation of social wealth. This stagnation of the rate of capital accumulation, together with the expansion of the middle-class layer we're discussing, are in fact two sides of the same coin. Its members enjoy high incomes, but very few can or will pass down sizable capital through family trusts to coming generations.

Instead, this self-designated "enlightened meritocracy" is determined to con the world into accepting the myth that the economic and social advancement of its members is just reward for their individual intelligence, education, and "service." Its members truly believe that their "brightness," their "quickness," their "contributions to public life," their "sacrifices" (they humbly point out they could be making a lot more in business or banking) give them the right to make decisions, to administer and "regulate" society for the bourgeoisie—on behalf of what they claim to be the interests of "the people."

In exchange they get bigger and better homes, obscenely expensive K-through-16-plus education for their bloodline, high-end consumer "necessities," plus the equivalent of a "law-enforcement discount" on all major financial transactions. (The killing the Obamas made in acquiring their Hyde Park manse and grounds in Chicago, generously subsidized by a big-time Daley machine fund-raiser, is but one example typical of these milieus—plain-old graft and corruption dressed up in more upscale attire. Hillary Clinton's one-day bonanza in cattle futures while first lady of Arkansas is another.)

And believe it or not, these bourgeois wannabes see all these "rewards" as social sophistication, not the conspicuous consumption of schlock.

While the existence and expansion of these strata are largely divorced from the production process, they are very much bound up with the production and reproduction of *capitalist social relations*. They have a *parasitic* existence. To maintain their high incomes and living standards, they are dependent on skimming off a portion of surplus value—"rents"—produced by working people and appropriated by the bourgeoisie. Yet the big majority contribute nothing themselves to the creation of that value, even in wasteful or socially harmful ways.

Instead, many of them pursue careers—in the universities, the media, "think tanks," and elsewhere—that generate ideological rationalizations for class exploitation and inequality (as they strive to "reform" it, of course). Others, whether as highly paid supervisory personnel, staffers, or attorneys, administer the rulers' efforts through foundations, "advocacy groups," NGOs, charities, and other "nonprofit" institutions, here and around the world, to postpone and buffer the explosive social and political responses by working people to our worsening living and job conditions.

(The union officialdom, despite their petty-bourgeois lifestyles and bourgeois outlook, is not really a part of this layer. They are still too connected, just by the character of their dues base and function in capitalist society, to the grit and grime of working a job.)

The meritocracy is a social layer that is insecure in its class position. It lacks the confidence exhibited by the bourgeoisie, even by the nouveau riche bourgeoisie. The propertied rulers—comprising only hundreds of families, not thousands—*are* a confident class (except during prerevolutionary crises or times of a rapidly accelerating breakdown of the capitalist order). Not only do they own, control, and hold the debt in perpetuity on the commanding heights of industry, banking, land, and trade. They also dominate the state and all aspects of social and political life, and finance the production of culture and the arts, including their "cutting edges."

The relatively new meritocratic social layer we're describing here—*it's millions, if not tens of millions* in the United States today—is *not* confident. To the contrary. Dependent on cadging from the capitalists a portion of the wealth created by the exploited producers, these privileged aspirants to bourgeois affluence nonetheless fear at some point being pushed back toward the conditions of the working classes.

On the one hand, due to their very size as a stratum of society they recognize that the rulers find them useful to bolster illusions in the supposedly limitless "careers open

"The capitalist rulers are pragmatic and cold-blooded. They do what they deem necessary to defend their profits, property, and above all their class dictatorship. They use their state power: their cops, courts, armed forces, currency, border controls."

JOHN MOORE/GETTY IMAGES

AP PHOTO/BUNYAMIN AYGUN

Above: US border cops arrest migrants crossing from Mexico in search of work, Rio Grande, Texas, December 2015. More than 350,000 were arrested at border that year.

Below: Part of wreckage of hospital in Kunduz, Afghanistan, bombed by US forces in October 2015. More than 40 were killed in what Pentagon excused as "human error."

to talent" under capitalism. At the same time, and despite their shameless self-promotion, many of them also suspect that since they serve no *essential* economic or political functions in the production and reproduction of surplus value, they live at the forbearance of the bourgeoisie. In the end, large numbers of them are expendable, especially at times of deepening social crisis.

The capitalist rulers are *utterly pragmatic* in their policies, and *utterly cold-blooded*. But they *do* have class policies. They do what they deem necessary to defend their profits, their property and its accompanying prerogatives, and above all their class dictatorship. They *use* that dictatorship—they *use* their state power: their cops, their courts, their armed forces, their currency, and their border controls.

In contrast, this "meritocratic" middle layer has no class policy course of its own. To the degree they commit themselves to a course of action—often camouflaged as caring, feeling, thoughtful, and above all very intelligent—such policies derive from the needs and demands of their bourgeois patrons.

Despite the Obama *campaign's* mantra of "change," for example, the Obama *administration* has relied on exactly the same top Wall Street bankers and financiers as its predecessors, in fact, the very same moneyed interests—even the same individuals in many cases—who have been the architects of today's grinding capitalist economic and financial crisis. And more than any other administration in the history of US imperialism, its foreign, military, and "domestic security" policies are stamped by deference to the top echelons of the professional officer corps of the US armed forces.

This is the social layer from which Barack Obama emerged. Not from the majority proletarian Black nationality. Not from the producing, entrepreneurial small-business milieu, the petty bourgeoisie. And not from the bourgeoisie. It is with the class interests and world outlook of this increasingly multinational "meritocracy" that Obama identifies.

The main public "persona" they affect is one of measured empathy, a veneer behind which lies social hypocrisy. They too "feel our pain" but lecture us—scold us—more than Bill Clinton ever tried to get away with. The main pretension is the clarity of their thought and skill at winning over their listeners ("Let me be clear. . . ."—one of Obama's signature phrases). What they can't be clear about is that they "feel our pain" less and less. The greater their frenzied empathy, the less their sympathy for the toiling masses worldwide.

They resent their vulnerability in face of the actual holders of capital. It rankles and instills in them a thinly veiled cynicism toward traditional bourgeois values such as patriotism, thrift, faith, and family (that is, values *promoted* by the bourgeoisie as essential mainstays of social order, not necessarily the typical attitudes, let alone behavior, of the propertied classes themselves). And since, as Marx and Engels explained more than a hundred fifty years ago, "The ideas of the ruling class are in every epoch the ruling ideas," such cynicism also puts this elect of "intelligence" and advantage at odds with the values and standards held by broad sections of the working class in the United States as well.

Like others in his social milieu—Caucasian, Black, Latino, or otherwise—Obama thinks of himself as a cosmopolitan in the way the dictionary defines the word: "*having wide international sophistication, worldly.*" Sharply different from straightforward bourgeois nationalism (often called "patriotism," to soften it).

After several primary victories for her husband, in early 2008, Michelle Obama said that "for the first time in my adult life I am proud of my country." Barack Obama himself initially decided not to sport an American flag lapel pin (a decision he later reversed as the contest with Hillary Clinton became nail-bitingly tight in Pennsylvania). And when the Democratic candidate spoke to a 200,000-strong crowd in Berlin in July 2008, he announced he was "a proud citizen of the United States and a fellow citizen of the world." The Republican right raised a hue and cry over each of these incidents, and—given what has long been deemed acceptable from the standpoint of their class—they had reason for complaint.

As president, of course, Obama soon demonstrated in Iraq, Afghanistan, Pakistan, North Korea, and elsewhere that his administration would unleash US imperialism's massive economic power and death-dealing military might to "defend" the national borders, currency, and broader interests of this country's ruling class. From there, the Obama administration went on to carry out the assault on Libya in 2011; stepped-up drone strikes across the Middle East, Central Asia, and the Horn of Africa; organized the cold-blooded assassination of Osama bin Laden; launched air strikes and deployed special forces in Syria; and more.

And despite criticism from certain (not all) sections of the Republican and his own Democratic parties, whoever replaces Obama in the White House in 2017 will mainly build on, not scrap, the policies he has pursued—the so-called Iran "nuclear agreement" and elevated place of Tehran in the US rulers' Mideast alliances; the recognition that Washington's fifty-five-year-long course to defeat the Cuban

Revolution had failed and it was "time to try something new"; the "Pacific pivot" and bolstering of US military and trading power in Asia; and renewed efforts at a "reset" with Russia. Those are US imperialism's foreign policies today, not a two-term jag by the Obama administration.

But Barack Obama and many others in the meritocracy do *not* consider themselves, first and foremost, Americans. Obama wasn't just playing to the crowd early in his first term when he told students during his June 2009 speech at Cairo University that, "Given our interdependence, any world order that elevates one nation or group of peoples over another will inevitably fail." That's part of the sanctimonious rationalization of the meritocracy's privileged social position not only in the United States but on the world stage.

That doesn't mean that those in this layer are internationalists, even bourgeois internationalists, much less proletarian internationalists. But the meritocrats *do* identify with their privileged social peers around the world. They *do* have a social identification with these layers; they share a mission. They *do* care what professors, NGO staffers, attorneys, and other "brights"[1] in Paris, Berlin, Rome,

---

1. In articles published in 2003 in several magazines, Daniel Dennett and Richard Dawkins—university professors of philosophy and evolutionary biology respectively, and both authors of quite profitable bestsellers among the recent crop of "atheist" books—proclaimed themselves the pioneers of a global "constituency" of "any individual whose worldview is free of supernatural or mystical forces and entities." ("We" all know who that is, *and isn't*, don't "we"?) In his original *New York Times* op-ed column, Dennett disingenuously protested: "Don't confuse the noun with the adjective: 'I'm a bright' is not a boast but a proud avowal of an inquisitive world view." So "proud" that when you register online to "self-identify as a Bright," Dennett's web site promises you confidentiality.—JB

and London think about them. They *do* rely on such support as a counterweight to what they consider the more "vulgar" ruling families at home, who ultimately dictate to the meritocrats the limits of what they will and will not do.

Above all, they are mortified to be identified with working people in the United States—Caucasian, Black, or Latino; native- or foreign-born. Their attitudes toward those who produce society's wealth—the foundation of all culture—extend from saccharine condescension to occasional and unscripted open contempt, as they lecture us on our manners and mores.

Above all, they fear someday being ruled by those they worry could become the "great mob": the toiling and producing majority. Obama, in fact, has sought to protect the meritocracy the world over from those perceived in his petty-bourgeois circles as ignorant, bad-tempered, flag-waving, gun-hugging, family-centered, religious—in fact, stupid—"populists."

It's a class question

This "meritocracy," for lack of a better term, is in large part what Richard J. Herrnstein and Charles Murray were describing in the mid-1990s in their book *The Bell Curve*. In it, they attempted to provide a "scientific" rationalization for the rapidly rising income and class privileges of this particular middle-class social stratum in the United States.

The authors wrote that while ideological differences, at least in words, would continue to distinguish "liberals" from "conservatives," and the "intellectuals" from the "the affluent" ("the affluent" being their lingo for the capitalist class and its top managers and professionals), these "old lines"

"Obama insists that Clinton's 1996 legislation abolishing 'welfare as we know it' must remain 'a centerpiece of social policy'—even as its brutal consequences are being magnified by capitalism's slow-burning depression."

Above: President Clinton signs law ending Aid to Families with Dependent Children. Two decades later, only 26 percent of families below official US poverty level are receiving cash assistance—down from 68 percent in 1996.

AP PHOTO/PAUL SANCYA

JOHN GRESS/REUTERS

"The meritocracy is mortified to be identified with working people—Caucasian, Black, or Latino. Their attitudes extend from saccharine condescension to occasional and unscripted contempt. Above all, they fear someday being ruled by the toiling majority."

Above: Hillary Clinton, campaigning in West Virginia, May 2016, apologizes to laid-off Bo Copely (far left) for earlier "misstatement." Clinton said in March that if elected president, she would "put a lot of coal miners and coal companies out of business to cut CO_2 emissions."

Below: President Barack Obama giving talk, Father's Day, during 2008 campaign, at Chicago's Apostolic Church of God. "Any fool can have a child," he said—blaming parents who are Black for social conditions facing their children today.

had in reality begun "to blur" on the most fundamental class questions. The authors of *The Bell Curve* write:

> There are theoretical interests and practical interests. The Stanford professor's best-selling book may be a diatribe against the punitive criminal justice system, but that doesn't mean that he doesn't vote with his feet to move to a safe neighborhood. Or his book may be a withering attack on outdated family norms, but that doesn't mean that he isn't acting like an old-fashioned father in looking after the interests of his children—and if that means sending his children to a lily-white private school so that they get a good education, so be it.
>
> Meanwhile, the man with the chain of shoe stores may be politically to the right of the Stanford professor, but he is looking for the same safe neighborhood and the same good schools for his children. . . . He and the professor may not be so far apart at all on how they want to live their own personal lives and how government might serve those joint and important interests.

What we can add—something Herrnstein and Murray already knew—is that neither the private school nor the "safe neighborhood" any longer needs to be "lily white." In fact, even well before *The Bell Curve* was published, that certainly was not the case for the middle-class Chicago neighborhood of Hyde Park from which Barack and Michelle Obama hailed, and where they sent their two daughters to a private elementary school at a combined tuition cost of nearly $40,000 a year (a total above the annual income of about half of all families in Chicago, and at least 40 percent of families in the United States).

It is Obama's comfortable immersion in this arrogant, self-congratulatory, and bourgeois-minded milieu that is responsible for the few "blunders" he made during the 2008 presidential campaign. In comparison to other Democratic and Republican primary candidates, Obama was cautious and disciplined during the campaign. He was determined not to let carelessness scotch his ambitions. That's why his slips are revealing.

There were his widely publicized remarks at a fund-raiser in April 2008, for example, where he was speaking to a small group of supporters at a home in San Francisco's exclusive Pacific Heights neighborhood. The Democratic candidate was so at ease in that company that he let down his guard. His class prejudices poured out for all to hear.

Working people in the small Pennsylvania towns where Obama had just been campaigning, he said, and in "a lot of small towns in the Midwest," have been seeing job opportunities decline for a long time. "They fell throughout the Clinton administration, and the Bush administration, and each successive administration has said that somehow these communities are going to regenerate, and they have not. And it's not surprising, then, they get bitter, they cling to guns or religion or antipathy to people who aren't like them or anti-immigrant sentiment or anti-trade sentiment as a way to explain their frustrations."

Working people, you see, may be "bitter," intolerant gun-huggers, bible-thumpers, and jingoists—but that's "not surprising," since we're so insular, beaten down, and demoralized! (By the way, isn't it hard to imagine a more insular "small town" than sections of San Francisco? Or Manhattan's

Upper West Side? Or Obama's own Hyde Park in Chicago?)

But Obama's words in Pacific Heights registered more than just a momentary "slip." That's been confirmed time and again throughout his presidency. For example, speaking in 2011 to another exclusive gathering of wealthy backers, this time in Brentwood, California, the Democratic president remarked contemptuously: "When I talk to ordinary folks, they are not always paying attention. If you ask them about Medicare, they'll say, 'I love that program but I wish government wouldn't get involved in it.'"

During Obama's January 2016 "State of the Union" address, with a thinly veiled observation about those attracted to Republican candidate Donald Trump, he said: "As frustration grows, there will be voices urging us to fall back into our respective tribes, to scapegoat fellow citizens who don't look like us, or pray like us, or vote like we do, or share the same background." (What "same background" do most workers, whatever our skin color, "share" with the big majority of those at top levels of the executive, judicial, and legislative branches of the US capitalist government today, and its proliferating "regulatory" agencies and bureaus?)

Bourgeois corruption of affirmative action

The fact that growing numbers in this "cognitive elite" social layer are African American today is something that would have been impossible thirty years ago. That testifies to the expansion of the Black middle class and the evolution of social attitudes we've already discussed.

By the latter half of the 1960s, the concept of equal justice under bourgeois law, fought for and more broadly codified through the mass civil rights struggles, had been extended to encompass explicit and transparent *quotas* in hiring, college admissions, and promotions—what came to be known as affirmative action. It helped break down barriers that had long blocked large numbers of African Americans from achieving such social status.

During those same years, the urban rebellions by proletarians who are Black in Harlem, Watts, Chicago, Newark, Detroit, and smaller cities all over the country—as well as the rise of Black nationalist consciousness and organizations—convinced the US rulers they had better concede something more than formal equality. At least for a time, they had to accept the need for quotas. The ground the working class had taken—including, in some cases, through our unions—was registered in victories such as the *Weber* decision in 1979.

Today the privileged middle-class layers the current president is part of are proud of being "color-blind" to a degree that is new to bourgeois society in the United States. The glue holding these layers together is not color but social class—or, to be more accurate, their entrenchment in *a certain section* of a social class. And it's not uncommon for some of those who are Black, Latino, or female to note that, in their own individual cases, *they* got where *they* are—or could have—without any need for affirmative action.

Born as a victory of the working class and of the mass struggle for Black rights, affirmative action was initially a course of action aimed at unifying working people and the oppressed, in order to strengthen our unions and our struggles against the employing class and its government. In a few short years, however, it had been substantially corrupted into a tool of capitalist division benefiting the most privileged layers of Blacks, women, and other oppressed sections of the population—those seeking advancement into the meritocracy. Its corresponding political expression has been the attempt to suppress civil debate through wielding the "political correctness" club so hated by working people and others—a class reaction 2016 presidential contender Donald Trump has capitalized on.

A large section of the bourgeoisie today considers what they call affirmative action—which has little to do with its original social and class content—as necessary to the maintenance and reproduction of stable bourgeois social relations. The main function of such measures as they've come to be applied by the bourgeoisie is to reinforce illusions in imperialist democracy (i.e., "even a Black man can become president of the United States"). They are used to further divide African Americans and other nationally oppressed layers along class lines, and to deepen resentments and divisions within the working class as a whole.

At the same time, as both the labor movement and the struggle for Black rights receded, the rulers began taking back ground they had been forced to concede. The Supreme Court handed down decisions that increasingly restricted—in the words of a January 1989 decision—"the use of an unyielding racial quota." Following another such Supreme Court ruling in 1995, the Clinton administration issued a memorandum calling for elimination of any program that creates "a quota," "preferences for unqualified individuals," or "reverse discrimination"—three longtime battle cries of opponents of hard-fought victories to strengthen working-class unity and solidarity, such as the *Weber* decision.

A 2003 Supreme Court decision, while conceding the University of Michigan Law School could continue to take discretionary measures to maintain "a diverse student body," ruled at the same time that "universities cannot establish quotas for members of certain racial or ethnic groups or

The *Weber* decision: A gain for the working class

In June 1979 the Supreme Court upheld a contract negotiated by the United Steelworkers of America with Kaiser Aluminum. In order to upgrade employment for those targeted by longstanding discrimination, the contract had established a quota that one-half of the places in a new job-training program would be reserved for Blacks and women. The court rejected claims by attorneys for Brian Weber, a worker at Kaiser's plant in Gramercy, Louisiana, that he had been illegally excluded from the training program because he was white.

Prior to that USWA contract, while 39 percent of workers at the Gramercy plant were African American, only five of 273 skilled jobs there had been held by Black workers, and none by women. At the time, socialist workers and others actively campaigned across the country and throughout the labor movement with the pamphlet *The Weber Case: New Threat to Affirmative Action; How Labor, Blacks, and Women Can Fight for Equal Rights and Jobs for All*. Published by Pathfinder Press, it cost 75¢.

put them on separate admissions tracks."

Communists and other vanguard workers unconditionally oppose the rollback of any gains workers have registered that have reduced racist and antiwoman patterns of hiring, promotions, firings, and college admissions. At the same time, we give no political support to the way in which the bourgeoisie has more and more often implemented what *they* call affirmative action over the past two

"Affirmative action was won by the Black movement and unions as a weapon to unify the working class. Class-conscious workers fight any rollback of gains that reduced racist and antiwoman discrimination. But we oppose how the rulers have corrupted it into a tool to benefit the most privileged layers."

JOHN COBEY/MILITANT

The Weber Case

New threat to affirmative action

Andy Rose

How labor, Blacks, and women can fight for equal rights and jobs for all

Above: Strikers picket Newport News, Virginia, shipyard, February 1979. Successful battle for Steelworkers union recognition registered strengthening of working class and labor movement as a result of Black rights victories.

Inset: Pamphlet socialist workers campaigned with in response to effort initiated by Kaiser Aluminum employee Brian Weber to eliminate affirmative action in union contract, arguing "reverse discrimination." Many unions defended contract measures, and in June 1979 Supreme Court rejected Weber's claims.

decades. If the class struggle does not advance, then gains such as the *Weber* decision are perverted over time by the very operations of capitalist social relations themselves, as they become programs that provide a golden key for some to enter an exclusive club further up the income rungs of US society.

So long as capitalist relations exist, the fight for *quotas* in hiring, promotions, and school admissions—that is, openly stated numerical targets or separate lists for those facing oppression based on their race or sex—will continue to be an indispensable element in forging class solidarity along the road toward the revolutionary fight by the working class to take state power, hold it, and aid those the world over fighting to do likewise.

Contempt for workers who are Black

What is so instructive about Barack Obama's class identification—and those of his milieu, regardless of race or sex— is not just a patronizing view of workers who are Caucasian. When it comes to workers who are Black, Obama's attitudes are just as contemptuous, if not more so.

Take, for example, his remarks on Father's Day in June 2008 at Chicago's Apostolic Church of God, which has an overwhelmingly African American congregation. Much of the news coverage of that church service focused on the Democratic candidate's remarks about absent fathers, but he said a lot more than that. He scolded members of the congregation not to "just sit in the house and watch 'SportsCenter'. . . . Replace the video game or the remote control with a book once in a while."

"Don't get carried away with that eighth-grade graduation," Obama said at the Chicago church. "You're *supposed*

Lenin on working-class fight against national oppression

In the opening decades of the twentieth century, Bolshevik leader V.I. Lenin, responding to the increasingly Russian chauvinist policies of a rising privileged social caste in the government and party apparatus of the young Soviet workers and peasants republic, explained the proletarian character of measures to overcome the legacy of national oppression in a workers state.

In a December 1922 letter to the upcoming Communist Party congress, Lenin wrote that internationalism "on the part of the oppressors or 'great' nations, as they are called (though they are great only in their violence, only great as bullies), must consist not only in the observance of the formal equality of nations but even in an inequality, through which the oppressor nation, the great nation, would compensate for the inequality which obtains in real life.

"Anybody who does not understand this has not grasped the real proletarian attitude to the national question; he is still essentially petty bourgeois in his point of view and is, therefore, sure to descend to the bourgeois point of view."[2]

to graduate from eighth grade." (It's less harmful to workers and farmers than getting carried away with a Yale or a Harvard law degree, but that's another question.)

And then he scornfully added, "We need fathers to rec-

---

2. From "Letter to the Congress" in *Lenin's Final Fight* (New York: Pathfinder, 1995, 2010), p. 240 [2015 printing]. Also in V.I. Lenin, *Collected Works*, vol. 36, p. 608.

ognize that responsibility doesn't just end at conception. That doesn't make you a father. What makes you a man is not the ability to have a child. Any fool can have a child. That doesn't make you a father. It's the courage to raise a child that makes you a father."

Too many fathers, Obama said, "have abandoned their responsibilities, acting like boys instead of men. And the foundations of our families are weaker because of it," he added. "You and I know how true this is in the African American community."

A few months earlier, again speaking to a largely African American audience, Obama had lectured those in attendance about feeding their children "cold Popeyes" for breakfast—unlike he and Michelle in the White House, we presume.

Comments like these are creepy. Obama was holding individual Black family members—not those who expropriate the wealth we create—primarily accountable for the quality of the education, nutrition, and health care their children receive. "If fathers are doing their part, . . ." he said, "then our government should meet them halfway." Halfway! And only "if."

This same patronizing, class-biased message of "personal responsibility" was central to Obama's remarks to the annual NAACP convention in New York in July 2009, six months after his inauguration. Just because "you're African American," and "the odds of growing up amid crime and gangs are higher," and "you live in a poor neighborhood," Obama said, "that's not a reason to get bad grades, that's not a reason to cut class, that's not a reason to give up on your education and drop out of school. . . . No excuses. No excuses."

Addressing himself to parents who are Black, Obama continued: "You can't just contract out parenting. For our kids to excel, we have to accept our responsibility to help them learn. That means putting away the Xbox, putting our kids to bed at a reasonable hour. . . . Our kids can't all aspire to be LeBron or Lil Wayne. I want them aspiring to be scientists and engineers, doctors and teachers, not just ballers and rappers."

Clinton, Obama: Dismantling 'welfare as we know it'

The hypocritical and fraudulent character of Obama's 2008 Fathers' Day lecture about "the foundations of our families" getting "weaker" became even clearer a few weeks later, when he took part in a televised presidential forum in southern California at the Saddleback Church of Rev. Rick Warren. When Warren asked him about "the most significant position you held ten years ago that you no longer hold today," Obama immediately pointed to his support for the abolition of Aid to Families with Dependent Children (AFDC) by the Clinton administration and Congress in 1996. Obama said that he "was much more concerned ten years ago when President Clinton initially signed the bill that this could have disastrous results."

But by August 2008—a few months before the November presidential election, and a few weeks before the explosion of the world financial crisis and its unfolding consequences for workers' jobs and conditions—Obama was "absolutely convinced" that Clinton's "welfare reform" had to remain "a centerpiece of any social policy."

Quite a contrast to the scathing indictment a decade

earlier by Daniel Patrick Moynihan, then the Democratic Party US Senator from New York. Speaking on the Senate floor in 1996, he called the law "the first step in dismantling the social contract that has been in place since at least the 1930s." (The "social contract"—that's how a bourgeois-academic-turned-politician talks about concessions wrested as by-products of the mass working-class struggles that forged the industrial unions.) In a 1996 letter to President Clinton, Moynihan went even further, labeling it "the most brutal act of social policy since Reconstruction"—he should have said since the bloody *defeat* of Reconstruction.

What have been the results since 1996 of what Obama called this liberal "centerpiece"? A 2015 report by the Center on Budget and Policy Priorities summarized the brutal consequences, an outcome magnified by the sharp contraction in the rate of growth of capitalist production and trade—the slow-burning depression, in fact—that opened in 2008.

Far from guaranteeing women productive jobs at good wages, those pushed off AFDC who've been lucky enough to find work of any kind have been forced into low-paying, nonunion jobs with little or no health, pension, or other benefits. By 2013 the percentage of single working-class mothers with jobs stood at 63 percent— exactly where it had been in 1996. That means 37 percent have *no jobs*, even jobs with miserable pay, conditions, and protections.

And families receiving cash relief under AFDC's successor—Temporary Assistance for Needy Families—have been cut by more than 60 percent over that period. Only 26 percent of families below the official US government poverty level were getting TANF cash assistance in 2013—down from 68 percent in 1996.

Shackled in debt

While the bourgeois-minded meritocracy has seen its average income rise sharply since the 1960s, there has been a stark deterioration over that same period in the living and working conditions of a growing majority of the proletariat of all skin colors. True, the gap in economic and social conditions between workers who are Caucasian and those who are Black has narrowed—but not because times have gotten better for most African Americans. The reason is that jobs, wages, and living standards *have declined* for a growing majority of workers of all skin colors.

The current Democratic administration and 2016 presidential contender Hillary Clinton crow that the official US government unemployment rate today is roughly half what it was at the high point in 2009, soon after Obama first took office. The US economy is "pretty darn great right now," Obama declared at a news conference in March 2016. But this "official" figure masks the true jobs crisis for workers today.

• The so-called "labor force participation rate"—the percentage of workers who are actually in the labor force today—has dropped since 2000 from more than 67 percent to roughly 63 percent. In numbers, that amounts to millions of workers who, against their will, are no longer in the labor force.

• The percentage of jobless workers counted by the US government as "long-term unemployed" (that is, without a job for twenty-seven weeks or longer) has jumped from a bit over 15 percent in 2009 to close to 28 percent today.

• Despite the fall in what is often called the government's "headline" unemployment rate, the figure for Blacks remains 75 to 80 percent higher than that for workers who are Caucasian. That gap has not closed.

"If the gap in economic and social conditions between workers who are Caucasian and those who are Black has narrowed since the 1960s, it's not because times have gotten so much better for most African Americans. The reason is that jobs, wages, and living standards have declined for a growing majority of workers of all skin colors."

Working people in the United States are also being hit hard by the disastrous consequences of the rulers' drive over the past several decades to float their rate of profit on a sea of debt, in which *we* are left to drown. How did this come about?

Since the late 1960s the capitalists have confronted renewed pressure on their average profit rate, which has gradually been trending down. The first post-1930s worldwide recession occurred in 1974–75. In face of this more than four-decade-long slowdown in capital accumulation, the rulers have held back expenditures for the expansion of productive capacity and large-scale employment of labor.

In hopes of boosting capital accumulation, the rulers' political servants in the White House and Congress, Democrats and Republican alike, together with the Federal Re-

> "Working people are being hit hard by the rulers' drive to float their profits on a sea of debt in which *we* are left to drown."

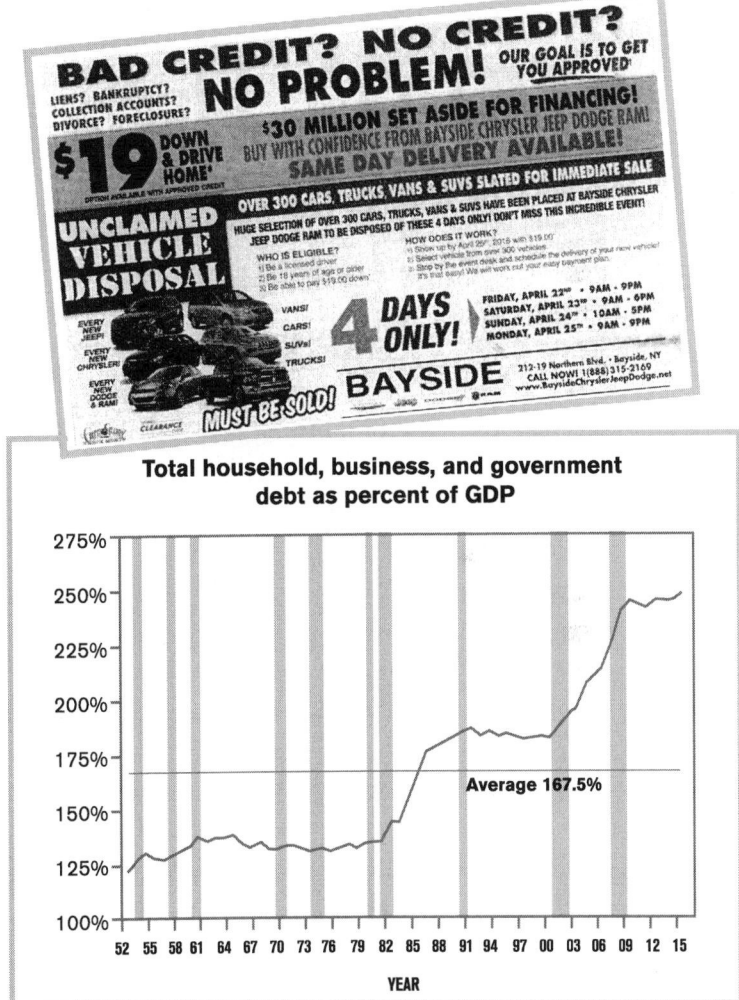

Source: Federal Reserve Board, Bureau of Economic Analysis, through Q4 2015

Top: Ad in *New York Daily News*, April 2016. US rulers have "goaded and lured growing layers of workers into credit card debt, student loans, auto 'financing,' and mortgages."

serve Board, massively expanded the use of credit. They flushed trillions of dollars into banks across the imperialist financial system and encouraged a degree of leverage that would make Las Vegas blush.

Among the earliest targets of the banks, going back to the 1980s, were oppressed nations across Latin America, Africa, and Asia, as well as working farmers in the United States. Capitalist governments in the semicolonial world were increasingly pushed toward default (and toward ruthlessly squeezing the toilers), while farmers in the US were driven into foreclosure and loss of the land they tilled.

The US rulers also simultaneously goaded and lured growing layers of the working class into deep indebtedness—credit card debt, student loans, auto "financing," mortgages and "home equity loans." With real wages declining, growing numbers of us have little or nothing left at the end of the month to pay off interest and principal on loans. We can't pay the bills.

To paraphrase the old Tennessee Ernie Ford song, more and more workers "owe our souls to the company store."

Pushing "home ownership" became one of the capitalists' favorite ways of shackling working people with debt. Both the Clinton and George W. Bush administrations unrelentingly pressed workers to take on what became known as "subprime" loans to buy houses and apartments—"low-down-payment" (or even "no-down-payment") loans, "adjustable rate" financing, and other forms of high-risk debt servitude. Banks solicited what cynically came to be called "liars' loans." (That is, the lender and borrower exchanged mutual winks when filling out mortgage applications. Debtors, of course, eventually got crushed, while bankers made out like bandits.) This drive accelerated to a dizzying degree before it came crashing down in 2007–08, with millions of working-class families losing their houses.

"The great mortgage 'bargains' had a political benefit for the ruling families. Under capitalism owning a house fosters the illusion that we too are 'property-holders' with a stake in the capitalist system. It subverts our class solidarity by elevating relations with 'fellow owners' over those with fellow workers."

The great house-purchase "bargains" had a class *political* benefit for the ruling families, too. They recognize that under capitalism, owning a house has a conservatizing impact on workers and the oppressed. It fosters the illusion that we too are "property holders," with a stake in the capitalist system.

As former Federal Reserve Board chairman Alan Greenspan candidly wrote in 2007: "I was aware that the loosening of mortgage credit terms for subprime borrowers increased financial risk, and that subsidized home ownership initiatives distort market outcomes. But I believed then, as now, that the benefits of broadened home ownership are worth the risk [*for the rulers!*—JB]. Protection of property rights, so critical to a market economy, requires a critical mass of owners to sustain political support."[3]

---

3. Alan Greenspan, *The Age of Turbulence: Adventures in a New World* (New York: Penguin, 2007), p. 233.

Owning a house ties workers down with onerous mortgage payments and endless expenditures of time and money for physical upkeep and repairs. It subverts our habits of class solidarity by elevating relations and problems we share in common with "fellow owners," fellow "property-holding taxpayers," over those with fellow workers.

It makes us less footloose. It makes us less *free*, as Engels insisted—more tied to the land the "real estate" rests on. In his 1873 booklet *The Housing Question*, Engels explained that a title to real property (sentimentally called "home" ownership by its bourgeois proponents who, with consummate cynicism, add a maudlin touch to all their demagogy) is "a fetter" for workers in capitalist society. "Give them their own houses, chain them once again to the soil, and break their power of resistance" during "a big strike or a general industrial crisis," Engels wrote.[4]

By-products of working-class struggle

Among the by-products of the working-class battles that built the industrial unions in the 1930s, and of the proletarian-led struggle for Black rights in the 1950s and 1960s, are government programs the working class depends on in addition to what we're paid in wages by an employer, whether private or government.

Social Security pensions, for example, were conceded by the capitalist rulers in 1935 as big labor battles were on the rise. Medicare and Medicaid were established in 1965 as a

4. Frederick Engels, "The Housing Question," in *Collected Works*, vol. 23, p. 344.

"Among the by-products of the working-class battles that built the industrial unions in the 1930s, and of the proletarian-led struggle for Black rights in the 1950s and 1960s, are government programs—like Social Security—workers depend on in addition to what we're paid in wages by an employer."

MINNESOTA HISTORICAL SOCIETY

LIBRARY OF CONGRESS

Top: Militant strikes won by Teamsters in Minneapolis, Minnesota, in 1934, along with actions by California dockworkers and Ohio auto workers, opened way for workers throughout basic industry to forge unions.

Bottom: 15,000 demonstrate in Harlem, March 1965, in solidarity with voting-rights protests in Selma, Alabama, where police brutally assaulted marchers.

direct result of pressure from the movement that brought down Jim Crow and the urban uprisings that turned the country and the confidence of the ruling class upside down. And in 1972 the Supplemental Security Income (SSI) program for the blind, disabled, and elderly was established, a further consequence of those struggles.

The Social Security Act of 1935 had included small retirement supplements for many workers, federally mandated unemployment insurance and workers compensation, and aid for dependent children (paid to eligible mothers). This legislation was crafted by the Roosevelt administration to serve the needs of capital by *limiting* concessions as much as possible. For example, not only were retirement benefits financed in part by a payroll tax on workers (a regressive, anti-working-class measure), but the minimal sums paid out were meant only as a minor supplement to whatever workers were able to put aside for old age (usually nothing) or get from their adult sons and daughters.

What's more, since average life expectancy in 1935 was below sixty-two, and just below sixty for men, the anticipated government payout on pension benefits beginning at age sixty-five would be small—in fact, in close to a majority of cases, nary a penny!

Social Security payments were not intended to defend and strengthen the working class. They returned to workers no more than a token of the wealth produced by our social labor. Social Security was aimed at bolstering the responsibility of families for meeting the needs of the young, the elderly, the disabled, and the ill, including reinforcing the social norm that the place of working-class women with dependent children was in the home. (I say working-class women, because the bourgeois family has always hired or retained a phalanx of wet nurses, nannies, tutors, and even dog-walkers—in the latter case, the comical twenty-first century surrogate for the old bourgeois stable staff.)

"Only when capitalist social relations are uprooted through working-class action along the road to the conquest of state power—only when economic compulsion, the wages system, ceases to be the foundation of all social interaction—will new human relations emerge."

All sanctimonious prattle by the capitalist rulers and their spokespersons about "defending the working-class family" serves only as a means of absolving the propertied ruling families and their government institutions of *social* responsibility for food and clothing, education, health care, housing, transportation, and more. It's the banner under which these responsibilities are pressed on individual workers—that is, primarily on women.

It is these capitalist social relations that are the root of so much individual and family misery today. Only when they are uprooted through revolutionary action by the working classes along the road to the conquest of state power—only when economic compulsion, the wages system, the "cash nexus," cease to be the foundation of all social interaction—will new human relations eventually emerge.

Working people and our unions have a vital stake not only in defending what we've fought for and won from the employing class, but above all in building a mass social and political movement of the working class *to extend these conquests as universal rights*—not means-tested charity—*for all*. Through our labor, the working class, in this country and worldwide, produces more than enough wealth to provide education, health care, housing, and retirement to every human being on earth, for a lifetime.

Every move toward a "family-centered" social policy, instead of an independent proletarian course to advance the historic interests of working people, including the right of every woman to reproductive freedom . . .

Every step by "talented" youth from the working class toward "a career" as a ladder up (and *out* of their class) . . .

Every move toward state-funded and "faith-based" charity (and the Obama administration has followed in Bush's footsteps on the latter), instead of government-guaranteed education, health care, and pensions as *the universal social rights of the working class* . . .

Every move toward tightening the trap of mortgage-debt slavery (that is, "home ownership" under capitalism), as opposed to a revolutionary social movement of the toilers that demands nationalization of the land and the housing stock as we fight for pleasant, spacious, and affordable accommodations for all . . .

Every such move weakens the working class and labor movement, as it strengthens the hand of the rulers, who seek to blame sections of our class and other scapegoats for the accelerating ills of the world capitalist order.

Every such move strikes a blow to what working people, including Blacks, women, and the foreign born, have fought for and conquered from the Civil War and Radical

Reconstruction on—through the mass social movement that built the industrial unions, and the Black-led struggles of the 1950s, 1960s, and early 1970s that drove a stake through the heart of Jim Crow and deeply benefited all working people in the United States.

Capitalism, the working class, and the transformation of learning

"Man truly reaches his full human condition when he produces without being compelled by physical necessity to sell himself as a commodity."

—*Ernesto Che Guevara*

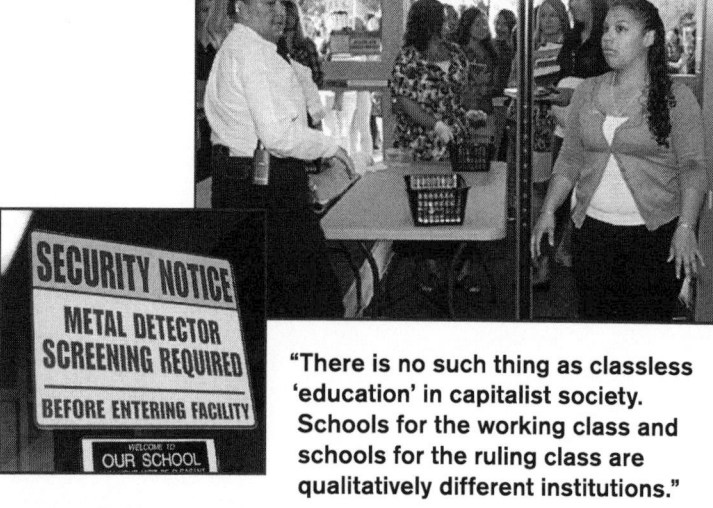

"There is no such thing as classless 'education' in capitalist society. Schools for the working class and schools for the ruling class are qualitatively different institutions."

Top: Assembling trucks in Navistar plant, Ohio, 2014.

Bottom: In many US schools, classes start with lines to pass through metal detectors. Here, high school in Hazleton, PA, August 2012.

Capitalism, the working class, and the transformation of learning

GERARDO SÁNCHEZ: One thing I sometimes have a hard time explaining to interested students when I set up literature tables on campus is why they should support union struggles. Some of them say, for instance, that a lot of workers take home higher pay than some college graduates end up making.

"Why should I go to school, pay $30,000 or whatever before graduating, and then get a job making $7 or $8 an hour," some students ask, "while mine workers, autoworkers, and other union members make $12 or $15 an hour [$20 to $25 in 2016 dollars]? Workers don't have a college education and I do. Why should I support their strike when

The exchange printed here took place during the discussion period following a talk by Jack Barnes at a socialist educational conference held in Greensboro, North Carolina, on April 10, 1993. It was first published in *Capitalism's World Disorder*, a collection of talks by Barnes that appeared in 1999, and republished on its own in 2000 as *The Working Class and the Transformation of Learning: The Fraud of Education Reform under Capitalism*. Translated into half a dozen other languages (Spanish, French, Farsi, Greek, Swedish, and Icelandic), more than 20,000 copies of the pamphlet have been sold worldwide.

they make so much money already?"

I find that some young people think there is no future for them once they graduate, and are swayed by these kinds of bourgeois, right-wing antiunion positions. Could you say something about this?

JACK BARNES: Among other things, the students you describe have an exaggerated notion about what the average worker earns, including unionized workers. They also seem to be mystified by two false notions.

First, that there is some connection between actual skills imparted in a college education and the income of college graduates. There is none.

Second, that there is some kind of "income pie" that is fixed, whereby a group of workers winning higher wages means lower incomes for everybody else. That is a myth promoted by the capitalists to protect their profits and profit rates by seeking to turn working people against one another.

The truth is that wages have nothing to do with the value of what workers produce or a service we perform. To a substantial degree, wages are determined by what the working class, through organization and struggle, has been able to establish and defend over time as the socially acceptable minimum standard of living. That's what Karl Marx was referring to when he wrote in *Capital* that in contrast with "other commodities, the determination of the value of labour-power contains a historical and moral element."[1]

A fight by the labor movement to increase wages, including the federal minimum wage, creates a better relationship of class forces for all workers to win better pay and safer

1. Karl Marx, *Capital* (New York: Penguin, 1976), vol. 1, p. 275.

job conditions. And if workers under capitalism aren't organized into unions in order to defend and advance their class interests, Frederick Engels explained in 1881, then they won't "receive even what is [their] due according to the rules of the wages system."[2]

"The purpose of education in class society is not to educate. It is to give 'the educated' a stake in thinking they are going to be different than—better than—other people who work all their lives."

These are class questions, not questions of an individual's level of schooling. The purpose of education in class society is not to educate. The purpose of education is to give "the educated" a stake in thinking they are going to be different—better off, more "white collar"—than other people who work all their lives. In the process, the rulers hope to make those who manage to get a college degree more dependable supporters of the status quo. They want you to be comfortable supervising, "orienting," and testing workers—directly and indirectly. They want to be able to count on you as a stable supporter of the capitalist system. It is not education; it is confusion and corruption.

Entire social layers—lawyers and other so-called professionals—receive very high incomes just because they can hang a piece of paper on the wall, a piece of paper kept scarce by the action of the state. Due to the corner they hold

---

2. "The Wages System," in Marx and Engels, *Collected Works*, vol. 24, p. 380.

on these functions in the class structure and pecking order of capitalist society, these professional and other middle layers collect a "rent," a payoff, from the bourgeoisie. They live off a portion of the fruits of the exploitation of workers, working farmers, and other toiling producers.

That's another function of education under capitalism. It gives certain privileged social layers a *license* to a higher income—a *license* to a slice of the surplus value workers create through our labor. The surplus value we create is much greater than the wages capitalists pay us. In addition to the shares of surplus value the owners of industrial, banking, commercial, and land-owning capital divvy up among themselves (through competition) in the form of profits, interest, and rent, they also pay out part of this wealth to these layers of professionals, managers, and supervisory personnel.

In the big majority of cases, these individuals contribute nothing to production. But they *do* help the propertied ruling families maintain and reproduce the class relations, privilege, and domination necessary for bourgeois rule.

So the relationship between education and income in capitalist society has nothing to do with college graduates knowing more, let alone making a greater contribution to human welfare or creativity (or necessarily even a greater direct contribution to capitalist wealth, for that matter). Instead, it is a small price the propertied rulers pay for a middle class that helps them maintain social stability, hold off working-class demands, and rationalize the polarizing social consequences of the relations of production under capitalism.

Liberals, for example, have recently made a lot of noise about figures showing that the gap has grown over the past fifteen years between the average annual incomes of high school and college graduates. Does that mean college graduates have gotten that much smarter over the past decade and a half, or that their skills are in that much greater demand by the capitalists? Does it mean that hi-tech society today has a greater need for "symbolic analysts" than it does for "routine producers," as Clinton's secretary of labor, Harvard professor Robert Reich, would have us believe?

"Until society is reorganized so that education is a human activity from the time we are very young until the time we die, there will be no education worthy of working, creating humanity. Social solidarity will never exist."

No, this growing income gap means the union movement has gotten weaker and real wages have been pushed down. The price of our labor power has been driven down by the bosses. That's all it means.

Nor is there a fixed income pie. Higher wages won by workers mean lower profits for capitalists; they don't come out of a "wage pool" that's depleted to the detriment of other workers and the lower middle class. In fact, higher wages and better conditions won in struggle by the labor movement put the working class as a whole—together with working farmers and other toiling allies—on a stronger footing to fight for better living standards and conditions of life and work. That's why the capitalists carry out an ideological offensive to convince the middle class and layers of workers of the false and reactionary view that wage hikes are the cause of everything from inflation to unemployment to outright impoverishment.

None of this is true. Marx explained this many years ago in his pamphlets *Wage-Labor and Capital* and *Wages, Price, and Profit* (subsequent editors changed the title to *Value, Price, and Profit*, but I am using Marx's title; it is more accurate). On this point, there is nothing to add to the basic analysis he offers in those pamphlets, which were written as political weapons for the workers movement a hundred plus years ago and remain just as valuable today.

Until society is reorganized so that education is a human activity from the time we are very young until the time we die, there will be no education worthy of working, creating humanity. There will only be the pretensions to education or to technical expertise of a small group of people. That is the historical truth.

Not a 'youth' question

Capitalist society promotes the myth that education is a youth question. But any society that sees education as a question just for young people can never have education that is meaningful for human beings, including youth. Social solidarity will never exist in such a society.

The working class cannot begin with how to change things so that *youth* get a better education. We have to begin with how to transform the values of society, not just the economics; it cannot be reduced simply to an economic problem. To be meaningful, education has to create the possibilities for society as a whole to advance, instead of reinforcing the exploitation of the majority by the few. Until then, the only "liberal education" available to any fighter who wants one is political education within the workers movement.

What is taught in most schools today is largely worthless. There are a handful of skills that provide some preparation for life—learning to read, learning to write, learning to compute, practicing to increase our attention spans, learning the discipline necessary to study and use our minds. Reading and studying are extremely hard. It takes discipline to sit still for three hours, two hours, even one hour—not moving, not jumping up—and to work through ideas. Working through ideas is hard; we all have to be taught how to do it—every one of us. But it is part of taking ourselves seriously. It is part of taking humanity seriously. We have to learn how to read and study by coming to better understand how other people live and work, whether they are older or younger than we are.

Most everything else we are taught in school, especially in the so-called social sciences and related "disciplines," are things we need to unlearn. Civics courses, social studies courses—these are all obfuscation. There is technical training of certain kinds, and applied sciences, that can be OK, with some luck. But these are forms of apprenticeships, not liberal education in the meaningful, universal sense.

Many young people wonder why they should go to school for twelve years in this society. Most never learn anything of value past the sixth or seventh grade. I went to working-class public schools in southern Ohio in the 1940s and 1950s. I never had to write a single essay or do anything like that my entire time in school; I was never given a reason to concentrate on doing so. But I had some teachers who were fine people and who encouraged me to read, taught me grammar and spelling, showed me by example how to at least sit quietly and work for a while. They displayed some social solidarity. That is all I can say I ever got from going to school. But that part turned out to be valuable. It was a lucky accident. But because of this accident, I learned to read, acquired the habit of reading, and acquired it for *life*. At the same time, I hated reading what they crammed down my throat in high school. I hated Shakespeare then; I hated *Macbeth* the way it was taught.

Most young people in capitalist society never get taught they have anything to look forward to after their compulsory schooling is over. They never get taught in such a way as to make them believe the educational system is based on the assumption that their lives are worth a damn. (Many of us can remember teachers and principals who reeked of this attitude, I'm sure.) Instead, young people in our society learn they have nothing to look forward to. They do not need to be told this in so many words; all they have to do is just watch other workers older than themselves. They just watch people like themselves who are above seventeen or eighteen years of age.

Between ages six and seventeen, the majority of young workers go to school six or seven hours a day; they are supposed to read books, work for good grades, study things, turn in homework. Then, all of a sudden they turn eighteen and they never do it again. First they are supposed to "just say no" to anything that is fun. Then they are supposed to just say *yes* to anything an employer demands.

Don't underestimate young people's moral yearnings, their openness, human solidarity, and sensitivity. Perhaps they cannot put what they see into words. Perhaps they cannot theorize it. But they *know* a lot about what's going on. What does the kind of education they get have to do with the human race?

To really discuss education is not to discuss how to reform the seventh grade in Canarsie. The seventh grade in Canarsie *is not going to be reformed*. Or in Louisville. Or anywhere else. I guarantee it, because the owners of property in the means of production in this society have no need, and thus no desire, for workers to be educated. It is not true that the capitalist class needs for workers to be educated; it's a lie. They need for us to be obedient, not to be educated. They need for us to have to work hard to make a living, not to be critical. They need for us to consume all we make each week buying their products. Above all, they need for us to lose any desire over time to broaden our scope and become citizens of the world.

These realities about what is called public education for the working class have their complement for the upper classes in both exclusive private and elite "public" schools. Long before Charles Murray and Richard Herrnstein wrote *The Bell Curve*—indeed, centuries beforehand—such schools inculcated the belief that workers are better off if we've internalized values accepting our station in life when we're young and "just say yes" to our "betters."

But the employing class doesn't need for us to be disciplined. Obedience on the job, yes; discipline in life, no. In fact, indiscipline in life puts us more in their grasp. That is what the employers want from the working class.

Most of you in the audience here tonight are workers. Do you have to be literate to do your job—not intelligent, but literate? Think about it. Do you have to be literate to work on the railroad? In an auto plant? Do you have to be literate to be a worker in an oil refinery? I don't think so; everything is color-coded, or number-coded. You don't need to be literate. Let alone be *educated*. Let alone have pride, self-respect, and initiative. Let alone to work together with fellow human beings to do things collectively, and to derive pleasure from it. That kind of education would be a danger for the rulers. Can you imagine people like *that*—fifteen, sixteen, seventeen, eighteen years old—coming into the workforce? They would take not only to union solidarity, but also to historical materialism and its revelatory and liberating character, like fish to water.

Only by looking at education this way can we understand the depth of the crisis. There is no meaningful education in this country under capitalism's school system, *and there won't be*. There will be some elementary reading, writing, and arithmetic. Certain people will be steered into technical specializations, and a few will be drawn over time into the lower ranks of better-off social layers, in order to demonstrate to all other workers that we don't "merit" being rewarded.

A thin layer of young people—most from economically privileged backgrounds, plus a handful of lucky individuals from the working class—will even be given a chance to find their way to more creative work. That is a very thin layer, however, one that everyone would love to be a part of.

Think seriously as a worker. How many of your co-workers are functionally illiterate? How many weren't when they started working but became so after ten or twenty years on the job, because there was no reason for them to read anymore? My father, a worker all his life, and a capable man, became *functionally* illiterate as he aged. Do the lives working people lead—the lives of those who create all the wealth, whose labor and imagination make everything possible, without whom the world would simply stop tomorrow—do their lives and their work encourage them to learn more each year? Is whatever leisure time workers in capitalist society have fought for and won as a class organized to encourage them to learn?

What do workers have to know for what they do on the job? It doesn't make any difference, does it? But in a society that is worth a damn, it *would* make a difference. There would be *continual* education. There would be a continual connection between work and education, between work and creativity, between work and works of art. Work would not be organized around competition to sell the labor power of our muscle and brains for eight hours a day to one of the highest bidders. And the greatest reward from work would be increased human solidarity, the pleasure and celebration that come from what we have accomplished together.

That is why the working class has such a stake in getting rid of the notion that education is a children's question instead of a *social* question. The former is a petty-bourgeois, sentimental cover-up for the true crisis of education. There will be no real education, including and above all for children, in a society where working people who are supposedly being educated know that a day will come when their education simply stops. Under those conditions, most young people grind away until that day comes—whether at age sixteen, seventeen, eighteen, or twenty-one; with or without a high school diploma. And then their "education" ends.

Work must become an activity through which a human being's desire to continually widen his or her scope—the desire to *educate* ourselves—can be realized. Professors and certain other professionals have something called a "sabbatical." It is a very good practice, even if it is often not used very well (that's another story that is not our concern). Every seven years, they take some time off— sometimes a half year at full pay, sometimes a full year at half pay. They go somewhere and study something new, broaden their experiences, improve their knowledge, meet people in other countries. That's the idea. Go to Italy, go to Japan, go to Mexico. Go to Asia, go to Nigeria, go to South Africa. It is a wonderful concept. Workers should have the same opportunity. Every worker should have a sabbatical every three years—get half the year off with pay to go to another country, or to another part of this country; to study something, to make further strides in another language, to enrich our solidarity. This can be a lifetime perspective.

Work should be the way Che Guevara talked and wrote about it during the early years of the Cuban Revolution—and what Fidel Castro and Che helped *mobilize* and *lead* as revolutionary organizers of that working-class government and communist party. Factories and other workplaces should be organized to promote continual requalification and ongoing education. In order to do that, "work must acquire a new status," Che wrote in 1965 in *Socialism and Man in Cuba*.

Along that road, Che said, a worker "starts to see himself reflected in his work and to understand his full stature as a human being through the object created, through the work accomplished. Work no longer entails surrendering a part of his being in the form of labor power sold, which no longer belongs to him. . . .

"We are doing everything possible to give work this new status of social duty," he wrote, "and to link it on the one side with the development of technology, which will create the conditions for greater freedom, and on the other side with voluntary work based on the Marxist appreciation that man truly reaches his full human condition when he produces without being compelled by physical necessity to sell himself as a commodity."[3]

When that day comes, then there will be something that can truly be called education. When that day comes, there will be links between the very young, the teenager, the adult, the older person—and they will be *human* links, *practical* links, *revolutionary* links.

No better reason for socialist revolution

In the US today, under capitalism, the only future we can count on is one in which education will worsen—in which education will fuel rather than retard social differentiation. There will only be "education" to squelch curiosity and creativity among the vast majority of youth, and to encourage escapism. There will only be "education" as regimentation. There will only be "education" as preparation to rationalize—or simply resent—class polarization.

I am not saying that everybody involved in education intends for this to happen. There are human beings in this society who are not communists and who are not workers but who genuinely, in their own way, would like to see children and other people have a better education and become more self-confident. I have had some teachers like that, as many of you have. But such individuals are not the norm, and they cannot and will not change the character of education in bourgeois society.

Instead, people are reduced under capitalism to hoping things will be different for *your* child. *Your* child *somehow* will get a decent education, *somehow* will get to college, *somehow* will not have the desire to learn beaten out

---

3. Ernesto Che Guevara, *Socialism and Man in Cuba* (New York: Pathfinder, 1989, 2009, pp. 17–18 [2015 printing]).

of them. *Your* child *somehow* will be able to compete with everybody else and have a better life.

That is what presidents of the United States do, isn't it? Bill Clinton was a good example. Clinton spent nine months campaigning about the importance of public education—and the whole working class knew what the Clintons were going to do when they had to choose a school for their daughter, Chelsea. They sent her to an exclusive, expensive private school in Washington. [The Obamas did the same.]

Class-conscious workers bear no resentment toward the Clintons because of those decisions. Envy of the propertied classes and their spokespersons is not a revolutionary or proletarian trait; it is encouraged not by communists but by anarchists and fascists. But in watching the president's family go about selecting a school for their daughters, thinking workers recognize further confirmation of two fundamental realities of class relations under capitalism. First, there is no connection between the values and public policies sanctimoniously espoused by the ruling layers and the lives they and their families lead. Second, there is no such thing as classless "education" in capitalist society; schools for the working class and schools for the ruling class are qualitatively different institutions.

If education is not discussed this way, then revolutionaries can never be convincing. If we start where reformers and liberals throughout the capitalist world begin—with *my* children, *my* neighborhood, *my* schools, *my* problems—then we get nowhere. And when the reformers start jabbering about defending *all* children, reach for your wallet and your watch! They are like the so-called right-to-lifers who defend children in the abstract before they are born, but oppose anything to advance a truly human life for most actual children from the moment they're born till the day they die.

There *is no universal education* under capitalism; there is no such thing as education "for all." There is only "education" for the working class, and a completely different kind of "education" for the small propertied minority.

If we do not explain education under capitalism as a class question (that is, from the standpoint of the bourgeoisie, two totally separate and unrelated questions for two different classes); if we do not present working-class schooling as the social destruction of human solidarity, as the organization of a society based on class differentiation, where human beings late in their teens become units of production in the minds of personnel managers and social planners; if we do not point to the fundamental issue of truly universal, lifetime learning—if we cannot explain education this way, then we cannot explain it at all.

But understood and explained correctly, there is no more important question for communists. Learning as a lifetime experience—I cannot think of a better reason to make a socialist revolution. What better reason to get rid of the capitalist state and use the workers state to begin transforming humanity, to begin building human solidarity? And we have the living example of the Cuban Revolution to show how it's possible to start down that road.

This approach to education is what we have to explain to students, to young people, and to others. If they went to school to get a leg up in life, then they did so due to a misunderstanding—unless they are from a class background that already gives them a leg up, and attended a school that teaches them they deserve it. But youth can be convinced of this working-class perspective, especially as they become active in a few political tussles, and if they

"Learning as a lifetime experience—what better reason to make a socialist revolution? . . . Explaining that is part of preparing the working class for the battle to throw off the self-image the rulers teach us, and to recognize we're capable of taking power and reorganizing society."

DAN FEIN/MILITANT

JANICE LYNN/MILITANT

Top: Alyson Kennedy (left), 2016 Socialist Workers Party candidate for US president, campaigning in Elmhurst, Illinois.

Bottom: Sam Manuel, SWP candidate for US Senate, joins fighters against police brutality at protest in Smyrna, Georgia, March 2016.

haven't yet been totally coarsened by this society. Young people want to match deeds and words. They still have vitality—they have not had it ground out of them. They can be attracted politically to the working class and communist politics, but only if we argue with them in this way.

Rightist movements, as I said, always try to play on the disappointments and resentments of youth from the lower middle classes or slightly better-off sections of the working class. That is one of the ways fascist movements are built. "You worked so hard for your education," they say. "Soon you'll be raising your children. And now *you're* going to have to pay more taxes for *their* children and *their* elderly." And the list of "thems" keeps growing.

Explaining the communist approach to learning is part of preparing the working class for the greatest of all battles in the years ahead—the battle to throw off the self-image the rulers teach us, and to recognize that we are capable of taking power and organizing society, as we collectively educate ourselves and learn the exploiters in the process.

INDEX

ALSO BY JACK BARNES

Malcolm X, Black Liberation, and the Road to Workers Power

"Don't start with Blacks as an oppressed nationality. Start with the vanguard place of workers who are Black in broad proletarian-led struggles in the United States. The record is mind-boggling. It's the strength and resilience, not the oppression, that bowls you over." —*Jack Barnes*. $20. Also in Spanish, French, Greek, Farsi, and Arabic.

Companion volume
The Changing Face of U.S. Politics

Working-Class Politics and the Trade Unions

$24. Also in Spanish, French, Greek, and Farsi.

Capitalism's World Disorder

Working-Class Politics at the Millennium

The social devastation and financial crises, the coarsening of politics, the cop brutality and acts of imperialist aggression accelerating around us—all are products not of something gone wrong with capitalism but of its lawful workings. Yet the future can be changed by the united struggle and selfless action of working people conscious of their power to transform the world. $25. Also in Spanish and French.

The Working Class and the Transformation of Learning

The Fraud of Education Reform under Capitalism

"Until society is reorganized so that education is a human activity from the time we are very young until the time we die, there will be no education worthy of working, creating humanity." Included in this volume. $3. Also in Spanish, French, Greek, and Farsi.

Is socialist revolution in the U.S. possible?

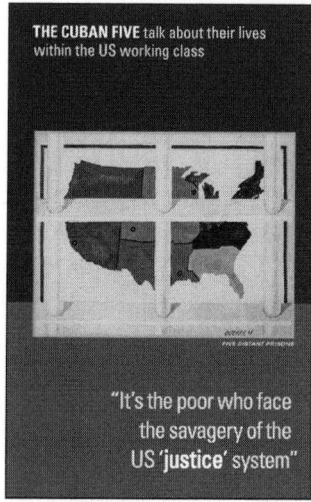

THE CUBAN FIVE talk about their lives within the US working class

"It's the poor who face the savagery of the US **'justice'** system"

"It's the Poor Who Face the Savagery of the US 'Justice' System"
The Cuban Five talk about their lives within the US working class
Five Cuban revolutionaries, framed up by the US government in 1998, spent up to sixteen years as part of the US working class behind bars. In this interview they talk about US capitalist society and its "justice" system. And about the future of the Cuban Revolution. $15. Also in Spanish.

50 Years of Covert Operations in the US
Washington's political police and the American working class
Larry Seigle, Farrell Dobbs, Steve Clark
Traces the decades-long fight by class-conscious workers against efforts to expand presidential powers and build the "national security" state essential to maintaining capitalist rule. $12. Also in Spanish and Farsi.

Socialism on Trial
Testimony at Minneapolis Sedition Trial
James P. Cannon
The revolutionary program of the working class, as presented in response to frame-up charges of "seditious conspiracy" in 1941, on the eve of US entry into World War II. The defendants were leaders of the Minneapolis labor movement and the Socialist Workers Party. Includes Cannon's answer to ultraleft critics. $16. Also in Spanish, French, and Farsi.

Teamster Politics
Farrell Dobbs

A central leader of the battles records how Minneapolis Teamster Local 544 combatted FBI and other government frame-ups in the 1930s; organized the unemployed; mobilized labor opposition to US imperialism's entry into World War II; and fought to lead labor and its allies on an independent working-class political course. $19. Also in Spanish.

The History of American Trotskyism, 1928–38
Report of a participant
James P. Cannon

"Trotskyism is not a new movement, a new doctrine," Cannon says, "but the restoration, the revival of genuine Marxism as it was expounded and practiced in the Russian revolution and in the early days of the Communist International." Twelve talks, given in 1942, on building a proletarian party in the United States. $22. Also in Spanish and French.

Is Socialist Revolution in the U.S. Possible?
A necessary debate
Mary-Alice Waters

Waters explains why revolutionary struggles by working people in the US are inevitable, forced upon us by the assaults of the propertied classes. As solidarity grows among working people, class battles can already be seen. $7. Also in Spanish, French, and Farsi.

Capitalism's Long Hot Winter Has Begun
Jack Barnes

Today's global capitalist crisis is the opening stage of decades of economic, financial, and social convulsions and class battles. Class-conscious workers confront this historic turning point for imperialism, drawing satisfaction from being "in their face" as we chart a revolutionary course to take power. In *New International* no. 12. $16. Also in Spanish, French, Greek, Farsi, and Arabic.

Revolutionary leaders

The Communist Manifesto
Karl Marx, Frederick Engels

Founding document of the modern revolutionary workers movement, published in 1848. Why communism is not a set of preconceived principles but the line of march of the working class toward power—a line of march "springing from an existing class struggle, a historical movement going on under our very eyes." $5. Also in Spanish, French, Farsi, and Arabic.

Lenin's Final Fight
Speeches and Writings, 1922–23
V.I. Lenin

In 1922 and 1923, V.I. Lenin, central leader of the world's first socialist revolution, waged what was to be his last political battle. At stake was whether that revolution, and the international movement it led, would remain on the proletarian-course that had brought workers and peasants to power in October 1917. $20. Also in Spanish and Greek.

The Revolution Betrayed
What Is the Soviet Union and Where Is It Going?
Leon Trotsky

In 1917 workers and peasants of Russia were the motor force for one of the deepest revolutions in history. Yet within ten years a political counterrevolution by a privileged social layer whose chief spokesperson was Joseph Stalin was being consolidated. The classic study of the Soviet workers state and its degeneration. $20. Also in Spanish, French, Farsi, and Greek.

... in their own words

Socialism and Man in Cuba
Ernesto Che Guevara, Fidel Castro

"Man truly reaches his full human condition when he produces without being compelled by physical necessity to sell himself as a commodity." $7. Also in Spanish, French, Farsi, and Greek.

Malcolm X Talks to Young People

"The young generation of whites, Blacks, browns, whatever else there is—you're living at a time of revolution," Malcolm said in December 1964. "And I for one will join in with anyone, I don't care what color you are, as long as you want to change this miserable condition that exists on this earth." Four talks and an interview given to young people in the last months of Malcolm's life. $15. Also in Spanish, French, Farsi, and Greek.

Cuba and Angola
Fighting for Africa's Freedom and Our Own
Fidel Castro, Raúl Castro, Nelson Mandela

In March 1988, the army of South Africa's apartheid regime was dealt a crushing defeat by Cuban, Angolan, and Namibian combatants in Angola. Here leaders and participants tell the story of the 16-year-long internationalist mission that strengthened the Cuban Revolution as well. $12. Also in Spanish.

Long View of History
George Novack

Revolutionary change is fundamental to social and cultural progress. This pamphlet explains why—and how the struggle by working people to end oppression and exploitation is a realistic perspective. $7. Also in Farsi.

WWW.PATHFINDERPRESS.COM

Puerto Rico: Independence Is a Necessity
Rafael Cancel Miranda

One of the five Puerto Rican Nationalists imprisoned by Washington for more than 25 years speaks out on the brutal reality of US colonial domination, the campaign to free Puerto Rican political prisoners, the example of Cuba's socialist revolution, and the ongoing struggle for independence. $6. Also in Spanish and Farsi.

Problems of Women's Liberation
Evelyn Reed

Explores the social and economic roots of women's oppression from prehistoric society to modern capitalism and points the road forward to emancipation. $15. Also in Farsi and Greek.

Maurice Bishop Speaks
The Grenada Revolution and Its Overthrow, 1979–83

The triumph of the 1979 revolution in the Caribbean island of Grenada had "importance for all struggles around the world," said Maurice Bishop, its central leader. Invaluable lessons from that workers and farmers government, overturned in a Stalinist-led coup in 1983. $25

We Are Heirs of the World's Revolutions
Speeches from the Burkina Faso Revolution, 1983–87
Thomas Sankara

The peasants and workers of this West African country established a popular revolutionary government and began to fight the hunger, illiteracy, and economic backwardness imposed by imperialist domination, and the oppression of women inherited from millennia of class society. Five speeches by the leader of this revolution. $10. Also in Spanish, French, and Farsi.

Cuba's Socialist Revolution

Women in Cuba
The Making of a Revolution Within the Revolution
Vilma Espín, Asela de los Santos, Yolanda Ferrer

The integration of women in the ranks and leadership of the Cuban Revolution was not an aberration. It was inseparably intertwined with the proletarian course of the leadership of the revolution from the start. This is the story of how that revolution transformed the women and men who made it. $20. Also in Spanish and Greek.

Women in Cuba
The making of a revolution within the revolution

From Santiago de Cuba and the Rebel Army, to the birth of the Federation of Cuban Women

Vilma Espín
Asela de los Santos
Yolanda Ferrer

The First and Second Declarations of Havana

Nowhere are the questions of revolutionary strategy that today confront men and women on the front lines of struggles in the Americas addressed with greater truthfulness and clarity than in these uncompromising indictments of imperialist plunder and "the exploitation of man by man." Adopted by million-strong assemblies of the Cuban people in 1960 and 1962. $10. Also in Spanish, French, Farsi, Arabic, and Greek.

Cuba and the Coming American Revolution
Jack Barnes

A book about the struggles of working people in the imperialist heartland, the youth attracted to them, and the example set by the Cuban people that revolution is not only necessary—it can be made. It is about the class struggle in the US, where the political capacities and revolutionary potential of workers and farmers are today as utterly discounted by the ruling powers as were those of the Cuban toilers. And just as wrongly. $10. Also in Spanish, French, and Farsi.

How Far We Slaves Have Come!
South Africa and Cuba in Today's World
Nelson Mandela, Fidel Castro

Speaking together in Cuba in 1991, Mandela and Castro discuss the importance for Africa of Cuba and Angola's 1988 victory over the invading US-backed South African army, and the resulting acceleration of the fight to bring down the racist apartheid system. $10. Also in Spanish and Farsi.